LEMONS
THE WORLD'S WORST CARS

LEMONS
THE WORLD'S WORST CARS

TIMOTHY JACOBS

SMITHMARK

Published by Smithmark Publishers
112 Madison Avenue
New York, New York 10016

Produced by
Brompton Books Corp.
15 Sherwood Place
Greenwich, CT 06830

ISBN 0-8317-5493-1

Printed in Hong Kong

10 9 8 7 6 5 4 3 2

Design and picture research by Tom Debolski
Editing and captions by Timothy Jacobs

*Page 1: A 1936 DeSoto Airflow coupe. The
sister line of the Chrysler Airflow, the
DeSoto suffered the same aesthetic failings.
This one is wearing a cosmetic nosepiece to
improve its looks.*
*Pages 2–3: A 1971 Ford Pinto. Mechanical
problems, plus a safety scandal, defeated
this bid by Ford Motor Company to be the
leader of the 1970s sub-compact car market.*
*These pages: A 1974 Chevrolet Vega hatch-
back coupe. The Vega competed directly
with the Pinto, and, strangely, suffered
many similar defects. Both cars were born of
the age of poor quality control.*

CONTENTS

THE WORLD'S WORST CARS

In the pages of this book, you will encounter some of the less-than-shining moments of the long pageant of automotive history. From the wreck of Joseph Cugnot's steam car in the 1760s to the General Motors, Ford and British Leyland quality control debacles of the 1970s; from the Chrysler Airflow to the Nash Airflyte to the notorious 'Flying Wombat'; and from would-be amphibians to flying cars and cars that *might have* flown, it's all here.

Webster's Dictionary defines 'worst' as 'the most unfavorable,' 'the most unsuitable,' 'the least efficient,' and so on. This text was written with the understanding that no automobile is *totally* bad. However, the cars in this volume were chosen for a number of reasons, only some of which are included in the above, and a few of which Webster may find to be indefinable—if not downright ineffable.

Further, our definition of 'worst' becomes a bit more complex as we explore the ramifications of automobile

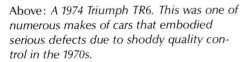
Above: *A 1974 Triumph TR6. This was one of numerous makes of cars that embodied serious defects due to shoddy quality control in the 1970s.*

manufacture from a historical perspective. Obviously, very primitive designs exist in a realm all their own, and we are left to discern the practicality of the design in terms of the technology of its time. Thus we can say that the 1763 Cugnot vehicle was, in a sense, a 'lemon' when we fail to detect an intelligent use of fulcrum principles that were well known at the time of its development.

In general, our task is made more interesting when a vehicle is carefully

designed, but its design would be altogether more suited for another usage than the one posited by the designer. Into this category fall 'crossover' vehicles—flying cars, amphibious cars and cars that were designed by men who yearned to design anything but a car. Such were the airplane-like Tropfen-Autos of the inventive Edmund Rumpler, and the Buck Rogers-style rocket car of the Hungerford Brothers.

In more common circumstances,

models that have otherwise reasonable designs contain so many production defects that they are either hazardous to drive, or impossibly expensive to keep running. Such was the case with many of the selections for our 'quality control' chapter on the 1970s. Automakers around the world have had their problems with this bugaboo from time to time.

More frustrating is the scenario in which an automaker achieves a design that is fresh, but which fails by dint of

being a compendium of features that *should have been* thoroughly worked out, one at a time. This was the case with the much-reviled Corvair, as well as the Chrysler Airflow—whose bodywork needed less *ambition*, and more *consideration*, in the design studio.

Occasionally, some designs are out of time, and are not necessarily good to begin with. Such was that archetypal failure, the Edsel. Manufacturers are burdened with selling such designs out of

Above: *A 1960 Chevrolet Corvair 700 four-door sedan. The Corvair's bathtub styling, rear-engine design and all-independent suspension struck a revolutionary note for the American auto market.*

The car was blighted by a compromised rear suspension design that made it a menace to drive.

Above: *A 1959 Edsel Ranger four-door sedan. The infamous Edsel grille is in evidence.*

Ford Motor Company took a big gamble on this car—and lost it all. The Edsel, a veritable symbol of 'lemonhood,' is, ironically, a prized collectors' car at present.

simple economic necessity—hoping that the public will buy enough of the unwanted vehicle to absorb some of the costs involved in producing the car.

Some cars are terrible safety risks. The glamorous Tatras of the 1930s contained hidden dangers in their sleek, aircraft-inspired styling. Fast and exhilarating, they were notoriously unstable at speed. On the other end of the scale, the humble Ford Pinto took over the 'unsafe' title from the Corvair in the 1970s.

Then again, other cars simply embody outrageous or unreasonable design, and some are so startling in their aesthetic approach that no amount of mechanical good can entice buyers to purchase them—here again, we have the Chrysler Airflow, as well as the ill-fated Phantom Corsair of the late 1930s, a car they called the 'Flying Wombat.' Nonetheless, some manufacturers have a stubborn tenacity with regard to outre designs, as was the case with the Nash Airflyte of the early 1950s.

The problem is, of course, that when an auto manufacturer makes mistakes, the customer pays with his money; per-

design strengths are sometimes brushed aside—and compromise is piled atop compromise, with plenty of room for error in the completed automobile.

Just so, while Milton Reeves felt that he was presenting a means to save on tires with his Octo- and Sexto-Autos, his own engineering myopia failed to take into account that the cars would not be easy to handle, despite all his own protestations to the contrary.

Therefore, this text is not offered as a pejorative listing, but rather as a cataloguing of all that can go wrong with even the best of beginnings. It may also serve to show that the boundaries of auto design have, at times, been expanded to include more than we may have thought.

My especial thanks goes to Mr Bill Yenne, whose commentary on flying car designs was of great usefulness in the writing of the present text.

Below: *A lowly Trabant. Trabants were built from 1958–90, with hardly a change in body or chassis design. The drive train was poorly designed to begin with, and the engine was extremely crude.*

Below, at bottom: *A rear view of a 1974 Pinto. Despite its 'econobox' design, this car is not a hatchback, although many Pintos were hatchbacks.*
Note the bulging sides—an attempt to maximize interior space that created a 'ready to burst' exterior appearance. This car was dangerous in rear-end collisions.

haps, if he depends upon the machine for his living, he pays with his livelihood; and ultimately, if the vehicle is simply unsafe, the customer may pay with his life.

Automakers hardly set out to create unsafe, unusable or inappropriate vehicles. Indeed, they often begin with the best of intentions. The Corvair, for instance, was born of a desire to introduce European-style panache to the American highway, and to do it at a reasonable cost. Unfortunately, in the corporate rush to turn a profit, original

THE HORSELESS CARRIAGES OF THE DAWN

1763 Cugnot steam vehicle

Leonardo Da Vinci invented a hand-cranked vehicle in 1490, and the mathematician Geronimo Cardano invented the universal joint in 1545. Christiaan Huygens invented an atmospheric piston engine in 1673 and James Watt patented the steam engine in 1769. Thus the story of mechanically-powered vehicles begins. Among the many brilliant successes that have come down to us are also ignominious failures and idiosyncratic departures from the mainstream that almost defy belief.

In fact, the story of the motorcar features an outstanding failure as one of its first true representatives. Nicholas Joseph Cugnot developed what is generally felt to be the first full-scale vehicle to be propelled by mechanical force.

Cugnot was a Swiss engineer, working for the French military in the eighteenth century. He was attempting to develop a military conveyance when he built his first vehicle. This steam-powered vehicle carried four passengers on its maiden voyage, and moved at a steady three mph (4.8 kph) until the boiler ran out of steam, which was every 12 minutes.

His second vehicle is better-known, however. It had a top speed of 2.5 mph (4.5 kph). This vehicle is still preserved in Paris, and is a wagon-like conveyance with three wheels.

The front wheel is both the steering and traction wheel, and the steam engine, with its boiler and twin 12.8 X 14.9-inch (325 X 378-mm) cylinders, is mounted upon the steering swivel with the front wheel. Steering this Cugnot wagon required great strength, as the full weight of the boiler and engine assembly is supported by the same armature that turns the front wheel. The difficulties of this setup are illustrated by the following accounts of the Cugnot vehicle in action.

An apocryphal account depicts Cugnot's vehicle snorting and whistling through the streets of Paris. As the barely controllable machine veered to-and-fro, the astonished citizenry alternately hooted, railed and shrieked in fright. Finally, Cugnot's arms gave out and his front-heavy monster plowed into a stone wall, knocking it down. Shortly thereafter, Cugnot was dragged from amidst the rubble, taken to jail, and his machine impounded before it could cause further harm.

Another story is generally accepted as being more accurate. The drive in question took place on private property, and no outraged citizens were present. The machine did, however, ram a wall, for which Cugnot had to pay a fine (we presume that he also had to rest his exhausted biceps and triceps for a day or so). The government cut off funding for the project, and that was the *coup de grace* for the Cugnot vehicle.

Further developments over the next century resulted in the establishment of the four-wheel internal combustion 'horseless carriage,' the development of which was rapid under the auspices of such as Gottlieb Daimler, Karl Benz and Henry Ford in the 1880s and 1890s. In general, such development segued neatly into the existing Machine Age milieu.

Opposite: The Cugnot Steam Vehicle of 1763, an invention that was both epochal and feckless. The machine shown here was actually Cugnot's second such conveyance (see text, this page).

Note the bulky boiler apparatus that bore down on the directional wheel, in defiance of mechanical principles that were even then well-known. The driver had to be possessed of simian strength to wrestle this cumbersome cart around a corner.

It was one of the world's first—and worst— motor vehicles.

1895 Burdick Springwound Car

Attempts to invent machines that, once started up, would run forever can be traced back hundreds of years, but no period in time saw such intensive speculation on the 'perpetual motion machine' as the latter half of the nineteenth century and the first half of the twentieth. Mankind had created the means of mechanically manufacturing items that previously had taken hours of exacting hand labor.

The problem of fueling such machines was a vital concern, and the plumes of black soot pouring forth from factory smokestacks had always been a source of discomfiture for most—but not for strictly environmental reasons. Financiers saw that smoke as money wasted, and wished for machines that needed fuel only to get started, and would not need fueling again.

Hence the *zeitgeist* was primed for everything from Rube Goldberg's cartoon extravaganzas that stretched the simplest action into a near-infinite series of events, to the experiments in thousands of backyard workshops to create machines that simply would never stop— 'perpetual motion machines.'

Of course, such principles would also be applied to that up-and-coming new machine of the turn of the century, the automobile. The extent to which perpetual motion—or at least non-fuel-burning—cars had seized the popular imagination is illustrated by a sampling of the entries in the Paris Horseless Carriage

Race (*Concours des Voitures sans Chevaux*) of 1894.

Among these were a vehicle 'to be propelled by weight of passengers'; another had a 'constant propulsion motor'; another ran under power of 'combined liquids'; and still another hoped to accelerate on a cybernetic-sounding combination of 'animate and mechanical motor.' While none of these exotic machines actually made it to the race, what counts is that they were conceived in some way, shape or form, and that was awesome (and perhaps terrible) enough.

Yet at least one similar idea came to fruition. In 1895, a Mr A Burdick (first name currently unknown), of Hubbell, Nebraska, designed a spring-wound car that could be wound by hand, or by a small electric motor. Beyond that, it was also possible to wind the car's spring by rolling it down a hill. Hence, this would be the ideal car for a landscape consisting of an infinite number of low mountains and small, shallow valleys. Any landscape more extravagant than that, and you'd overwind the car going down, and run out of power climbing up.

The hand-wind and electric motor-wind options notwithstanding, once the driver got the hang of the car's self-winding capability, the preferred choice was obvious. The Burdick Car was a noble attempt to remedy a situation that has been problematic since the first equestrian had to find fodder for his horse. In fact, had the ingenious Mr Burdick had a prescient grasp of mankind's present bondage to fossil fuels, he might have developed his Spring-Wound Car further. It's an idea whose time may yet come, given the proper terrain.

1897 Barsaleux

Even though there was a sense of fraternity due to opposition from those who still clung to the horse as the primary means of land travel, two schools existed among early auto designers. One school wanted to exploit the speed and novelty of the automobile as much as possible, without paying any attention to the shock that horses and teamsters felt when they encountered one of these 'horseless carriages' on the road. The other school felt that the public was owed a certain courtesy, and did everything they could to make the transition from horse-and-carriage to horseless carriage a smooth one.

This was, in fact, the first impetus behind the advent of the front-mounted engine, with the engine taking the place of the horse. Of course some inventors took it one step further, and attempted viable front-wheel drive vehicles, thereby

Below: *A cutaway view of the mechanism of the Burdick Springwound Car. While it was not quite a 'perpetual motion machine,' energizing this car was, under the right circumstances, easy as rolling down a hill.*

Of course, once one had rolled the Burdick Springwound Car down the hill, all the energy accumulated in the spring mechanism would be expended in climbing another hill to re-wind the car.

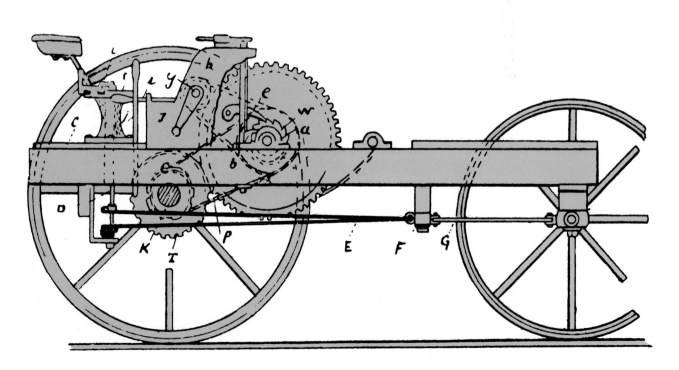

emulating 'horse-power' altogether.

Perhaps the ultimate in this emulative way of thinking was the product of Joseph Barsaleux. He invented a horseless carriage with five wheels. The fifth wheel was set out in front of the vehicle, and was the steering and drive wheel. Cloaking this drive/steering wheel was a full-size replica of a horse!

Needless to say, steering was by means of a brace and bit attached to the dummy horse's mouth. In a sense, the Barsaleux car was so odd that it was absolutely brilliant. After all, who could argue with such an open-hearted gesture?

1900 Woods 'Spider'

Among other attempts to soften the transition from horseflesh to cast iron were the 'horseless hansoms' of the turn of the century. A 'hansom' was a taxicab wherein the driver sat above and behind his passengers. None of the horseless hansoms were wildly successful, but as transitional vehicles, they were at least adequate—even though they lacked the *panache* of the genuine, horse-drawn hansom, with its sprightly hackney leading the way.

One of the less convenient examples of the horseless hansom was produced by the Woods Motor Vehicle Company of Chicago, a respected maker of electric

automobiles from 1899 to 1918. The cars built by this company had fine workmanship, and were elegant-looking vehicles. Perhaps none was so elegant in its general effect than the 'Spider,' a horseless hansom of 1900.

Of course, the driver sat above and behind the passengers. The Spider was powered by a small electric motor situated just forward of the rear wheels, and a chain or belt drive with differential pulleys was used to transmit the power.

The front wheels were used in steering, and the driver provided direction to same by use of a curved tiller. The tiller was matched to two long rods that ran along beneath the passengers' bench seat, and transmitted the driver's intention to the front wheels.

As with most cars of the period, this design, elegant as it was, had some flaws. One, it was not an easy vehicle to steer, because the driver was so far behind the center of gravity, and the steering apparatus was over-extended. The design was, after all, based on a horse-drawn vehicle. Carriage drivers had no trouble steering their vehicles, as the design was such that they sat behind the center of gravity: the power source—ie, the horse—was also that which was being guided, and the steering wheels would follow the horse in whatever direction it went.

The Spider driver, however, had to provide muscular power to move the front wheels right or left—a task that was made more difficult by the indirectness of the action. First, the tiller had to be

Above: *This illustration of a 1901 'front-wheel-drive' motor vehicle is very close to the basic mechanical design of the 1897 Barsaleux. Now imagine this front wheel and motor casement enshrouded with a stuffed horse—in much the same spirit as the horse's head adornment of the 'horseless carriage' at above left. That may approximate Joseph Barsaleux's ingenuously outrageous automotible.*

Above: *A Woods Electric Stanhope with an altogether more sensible design than that of the Woods Spider. The lady's slight smile evidences a wry look at what, after all, had to be a rather frigid experience.*

As the years rolled on, Woods electric cars came to resemble modern autos more closely. Even so, both of these passengers look like they would have preferred a real carriage to the uncertainties of this auto design.

moved to one side or the other, and this in turn transmitted force to the steering bars, which in turn transmitted energy to the front wheels.

For instance, in designs such as the 1900 Porter Stanhope, which was billed by its makers as 'The Perfect Automobile,' the driver at least sat closer to the front wheels than did the rear-positioned driver of the Spider. In this, he had the advantage of at least sitting over the wheels, and hence had more direct interaction with the steering of same — thus exerting more positive control. Later designs acquired the advantage of gearing and leverage combinations that made the steering of an automobile much easier and more accurate.

Meanwhile, the driver of the Woods Spider had to be contented with his somewhat difficult task. Then again, the Spider was designed for a stately pace, so the loose and inertially-frustrated steering mechanism did not have the dire

consequences it might have had in a faster car.

However, this was a convertible, and with the passenger hood up, the driver was consigned to peering through a small window in the rear of same for a glimpse at the road ahead. Naturally, the hood would be up most often at night, to protect against the cold; or in bad weather, to protect against the elements — both times the driver would need better vision, if anything.

One can imagine the driver hunching ever lower in his seat, attempting to peer past the headgear of a gaily-bonneted lady passenger, as the rain pours down his neck and runs off his hatbrim.

Woods eventually did see the light — both figuratively and literally. In 1901, they revised their design, and put the steering tiller up front, so that the driving was now up to one who had a better chance of seeing where the vehicle was going.

Somewhat more successful horseless hansoms were presented by the Riker Company of Elizabethport, New Jersey; and the Hautier Cab Company of Paris. The Hautier solved the obstructing passenger bonnet problem by positioning the driver so that his plane of vision was above the roof of the cab. Steering was still a bit of work, though. Hautiers were used extensively in turn-of-the-century Paris, the motoring capitol of the world at the time.

1903 Janvier

Nor was driver positioning the only question faced by early automakers. Though cars with four wheels seem so normal in the contemporary world that they are taken for granted, that configuration represents a solution to what was once a vexing problem. Some felt that three wheels were sufficient, and this indeed was a configuration that lasted for decades in the very popular Morgan

cycle-cars. It was, in fact, one of the first configurations worked out by Carl Benz, who manufactured a tricycle-car with a motor under its seat and a single directional wheel in 1885. This was a motorized cart with a front wheel instead of a horse.

The Morgan, on the other hand, presented two drive wheels to the road ahead and had one traction wheel behind. Then, of course, there were those who opted take the term 'horseless carriage' literally, and produced four-wheel vehicles with steering wheels in front. On across the design spectrum, then, were those who felt that more was better. For instance, if two drive wheels and two directional wheels were sufficient, why not make a good situation better with multiple drive wheels, and two directional wheels?

Such a vehicle was the Janvier, which was designed with the normal number of directional wheels, but had, like a modern armored car, no less than four drive wheels. This idea was not picked up by a wide range of other automakers, simply

Above: *An advertisement for Woods Motor Vehicles, featuring the Woods Spider. When the convertible top went up, the driver could not see the road ahead.*

Woods produced other questionable designs, such as the Electric Dos-a-Dos at left, top—another vehicle caught in the transition from horse to 'horseless' power. Even so, note that the driver's position is in the front seat here.

Left, bottom: *This turn-of-the-century Woods Electric Landau left the driver as exposed as the Woods Spider, but at least his field of view was unimpaired.*

The Selden brothers had a penchant for making their mark on the automotive world. Perhaps Arthur Selden was inspired by his brother George, who is shown, above, in the driver's seat of the car he invented in 1877.

George Selden based his notorious 'Road Steamer' patent on this car. He hoped to corner the market on automobiles for all time! He was ultimately unsuccessful, as was Arthur Selden with his unique automotive invention.

because the mechanism involved twice the parts that more conventional designs involved. This contributed to the possibility of mechanical breakdown, and also required more energy to operate, causing abnormally high fuel consumption.

Even so, this particular six-wheel configuration has been used with success for trucks, military transports and, generally, any application where extra traction and load-bearing are at a premium. It is not, however, a good configuration for general usage road cars.

1904 MacDuff Aeropinion/ Pneumoslito

Wheel and seating arrangements aside, there have always been a few brave souls who have sought to exploit relative development—inventions and ideas belonging to parallel disciplines. The case in point is that cars and airplanes developed almost side by side. It is only natural, then, that some crossover influences should appear in one vehicle or another.

Advanced styling incorporating aerodynamics was an early example of such influence—but some auto designers developed their vehicles with a much more literal intent. The MacDuff Aeropinion, in particular, was one of the earliest examples of a genre of cars that included

the Reese Aero-Car and the McLaughlin Maine-mobile. These cars used the propeller principle for motive power.

Sporting an aircraft-type propeller driven by a four-horsepower engine, the MacDuff Aeropinion could breeze along at 16 mph (25.7 kph). However, with a set of small wooden pieces fitted to its wheels, the MacDuff Aeropinion became the MacDuff Pneumoslito—a prop-driven sled! This was thought to be ideal for the seasonal changes that were endemic to the car's home town of Brooklyn, New York.

Ingenious (or silly) as it sounds, the MacDuff Aeropinion/Pneumoslito had a major drawback that, ironically, was the very thing that enabled its miraculous transformation from auto into sled—the propeller. While this whirling blade freed the car from the restrictions implied by the conventional transfer of torque through a drive wheel, it was also a potentially destructive force, should someone stumble into it.

The propeller was also outright destructive to the eardrums of MacDuff's passengers and those of any bystanders. Plus, the prop-wash from this auto would have deleterious effects on any traffic following it on the dusty roads of its day. A rainy day would pose a similar problem. This was a car that could literally 'blow you off the road.'

1908 Arthur Selden Car

Early automakers also explored other kinds of drive systems. For instance, front-wheel drive has long haunted the auto industry. Some recent examples have shown signs of conquering the problems inherent in this configuration, and it has generally become accepted with the advent of such successful front-wheel-drive makes as the SAAB, the Toronado and the Subaru.

In the 1920s and 1930s, there were, among others, the famous Cord cars that made front-wheel drive a feature of distinction—even if it hadn't been fully worked out, and was a troublesome feature on those fast and sophisticated automobiles. Also, one must not forget such valiant attempts as that of Joseph Barsaleux in the 1890s (please see the text on this vehicle).

The Arthur Selden Car was a first-decade attempt to apply the principles of pull, rather than push, to auto locomotion. Arthur Selden was the brother of George Selden—the very man who attempted an early monopoly on the motorcar, basing his claims on his 'Road Steamer' patent of 1877.

Perhaps encouraged by his brother's activities, Arthur commenced building his own original design in 1903. He did all the body and chassis work himself, and commissioned a two-cylinder, horizontally-opposed, air-cooled engine from the Brennan Motor Company of Syracuse, New York. The ignition was somewhat advanced for the time, being a jump-spark system, deriving its power from dry cell batteries.

A two-speed, planetary transmission conveyed power to the front wheels by means of a chain. The problem of allowing the front wheels to transmit torque as well as steer was solved by taking the burden of lateral movement off the wheels themselves, and transferring it to the body. In other words, this car had a steering hinge in its midsection.

It was truly a vehicle for corners, and *slow* corners at that. The fulcrum effect of having a rear half rolling toward the hinge, and a front half pulling away from it, must have resulted in some very nasty whiplash. This is not to mention the inevitable wear and tear on that hinge, which not only had to sustain side-to-side motion, but also had to support the weight of the midsection of the car.

Failure was awaiting the Selden brothers. There were no known buyers for Arthur Selden's car, and George Selden's try at monopoly was defeated by Henry Ford's 'Anti-Selden League' in 1911, when the US Patent Attorney annulled Selden's patent.

This page: *Views of the Arthur Selden Car of 1908. As can be seen here, the Selden Car resembled a Rube Goldberg device in its complexity of construction—and watch out for those turns!*

Note the chain-drive apparatus on the front end, and the bellows-like baffle that concealed the hinge on which this strange car turned.

THE WHEEL AND ENGINE WARS

1911 Reeves
Octo-Auto

On another side of the automobile design question, at least one automaker was rekindling the wheel-counting wars that had been earlier joined by the six-wheeled Janvier. Milton Reeves created the Octo-Auto, an eight-wheeled car, in an attempt to create a car with an especially smooth ride.

He reasoned that the famous Pullman railroad passenger cars rode so smoothly because they had eight wheels. He failed to note that the Pullman cars also travelled exclusively on the constant surface of a railroad track.

Therefore, the Octo-Auto rode very smoothly on very good roads (a rarity at the time) but was virtually uncontrollable on rough roads of the kind that then predominated, despite promotional materials stating that the Octo-Auto was absolutely the best car for rough-surface driving. Indeed, with its many sets of wheels creating eruptions of harmonic vibrations throughout the length of the car, the Reeves Octo-Auto became dangerously hard to maneuver on any but the *best* roads.

The extra sets of wheels were also touted as saving wear and tear on tires. Elbert Hubbard, who seemed to have had a commentary on everything in those days, came up with the absurd reasoning that, because the Octo-Auto had eight wheels instead of four, it should make tires last eight times longer! He also added much tongue-in-cheek testimony that the Octo-Auto was everything a

motorist could want, and was the smoothest and most practical car going.

The extra wheels added considerable weight to the car, which was armed with a middling-size four cylinder engine of mediocre power. Thus, getting rolling in this car was a bit like commencing a rail journey—the car took a while to build up steam. All that extra undercarriage equipment also added (contrary to Reeves' publicity) to the complications of any breakdown. It was an attention-getter, though: with so many wheels, it resembled a one-car parade.

Despite a personal appearance of the carmaker and his product at the Indianapolis Speedway in 1911, public interest in this veritable caterpillar of a car was not forthcoming.

Reeves was not one to give up, however. He came right back with a six-wheeled car, which he called, predictably enough, the Sexto-Auto. It was a case of 'still too many wheels,' and failed to distinguish itself in any other way than having a multiplicity of rolling surfaces. It was unveiled, and it failed, in 1912.

1916 Woods
Dual Power

Despite such occasional gaffes as the Spider, Woods enjoyed a solid reputation as a maker of electric autos. In the first decade of this century, electric cars were much in vogue, as the electric motor was far more advanced in its development than the internal combustion engine.

Hence, electrics were more reliable, and were innately more quiet—lacking the crude melange of mechanical noise and unexpected backfirings of the then-primitive gasoline engines. Electrics were also far cleaner, as they gave off no exhaust fumes, and there was no sooty buildup from such.

However, the gasoline engine allowed more freedom, having a comparatively more flexible power source than the electrics. Electric cars ultimately failed because their batteries did not allow the range that a tank of gas allowed internal combustion-type cars. The average electric car could cover only 40 to 60 miles (64 to 96 km) before needing a recharge.

Also, the batteries needed to power an electric car were massive, and added hundreds of inert kilograms/pounds to the car's weight. While some electric car owners had their own recharging units at home, most—especially in urban areas—

The 1916 Woods Dual Power car, an illustration of which is shown below, was a compromise aimed at keeping electric autos viable in the marketplace. With electric and internal-combustion engines, it had a heavy load to carry, indeed.

left their cars overnight in commercial garages, where the batteries were recharged.

In about 1912, due to steady improvement in internal combustion engine design, the average ratio of usable power time between freshly charged electrics and freshly fueled gasoline-powered cars became 15/40 in favor of the gasoline cars.

The public noticed this in terms of who was driving most—gas car owners or electric car owners. Soon, even the electric car's chief market—genteel ladies who appreciate the clean, quiet smooth-

to carry its heavy electric-power equipment. With two power plants aboard, this was a car that had more weight than efficiency. Woods discontinued the model within a year, and went out of business altogether in 1918.

1916–20 Le Zebre

Extra wheels notwithstanding, makers of internal combustion-powered autos had enough on their hands—so much

ness of the electrics—grew weary of recharging batteries. Gasoline cars, growing more sophisticated, would soon emulate the electrics' smoothness.

Woods Motor Vehicle Company saw the future and tried to do something about it. In 1916, they brought out the Woods Dual Power, an automobile that may have repercussions for the present fossil-fuel-entangled age. This interesting car had a four-cylinder gasoline engine and the standard Woods electric engine. The gasoline engine was used for starting, and for operating at speeds up to 15 mph (24 kph) if one so desired. Even more significantly, it was also used for charging the batteries for the electric motor.

The Woods Dual Power was an unfortunately cumbersome machine. Not only did it bear the weight of the electric motor and its batteries, it also carried the weight of an entire internal combustion engine setup. Therefore, it lost ground in either mode, consuming extra battery power carrying the gas engine apparatus, and consuming extra gasoline in having

so, that one seldom thinks of quality control in those early years. Yet, such makes as Pierce-Arrow, Cadillac and Rolls-Royce had already established the upper reaches of finish and soundness of construction. While such popular songs as 'He'll Have to Get Under/ Get Out and Under/ To Fix Up His Automobile' related the woes met by the owner of the average car of the time, most such autos were simply temperamental, and a few minutes of soiling one's shirt under the car would get the vehicle rolling again.

However, the make known as Le Zebre was, in its own humble way, a portable disaster. That this pitiable little car greatly resembled the idiosyncratic 1924 Amilcar driven by Jacques Tati's Monsieur Hulot in *Monsieur Hulot's Holiday* is no surprise. The two cars had a designer in common—Jules Salomon, who should have excluded small cars from his otherwise successful design portfolio.

To begin with, Le Zebre had an inadvantageous drive train design: the engine, clutch housing and gearbox were cast in one unit. All too often, engine oil

An additional four wheels were what separated the 1911 Reeves Octo-Auto, shown above, from more conventional designs. Those wheels also separated it from success.

Shown here is Milton Reeves at the wheel of his invention, during a promotional stint in Indianapolis.

ran back through the clutch to the gearbox, and the unit had to be drained every 50 miles (80 km).

That in itself would be unfortunate, but not insurmountable. Le Zebre also tended to lose its wheel nuts in transit. Besides the obvious shock of having one or several of the car's wheels fly off on a public thoroughfare, there was the danger of personal injury; injury to an innocent bystander or a fellow motorist; and property damage suits resulting from destruction caused by the errant wheel or wheels—not to mention the automobile itself, as it careened out of control.

Le Zebre did have its odd dependability, however. Its axle shafts broke regularly every 200 miles (322 km). Altogether, this innocuous and sprightly-seeming little car was not for the light of spirit—unless such a person were seeking the depths of depression.

Perhaps its name was an allusion to the frequent occasions of darkness that punctuated the 'light' periods when it hadn't caused an accident. For the record, the first Le Zebre had a 37.5-cubic-inch (616 cc) single-cylinder, water-cooled engine developing six hp. This was mated to a two-speed transmission.

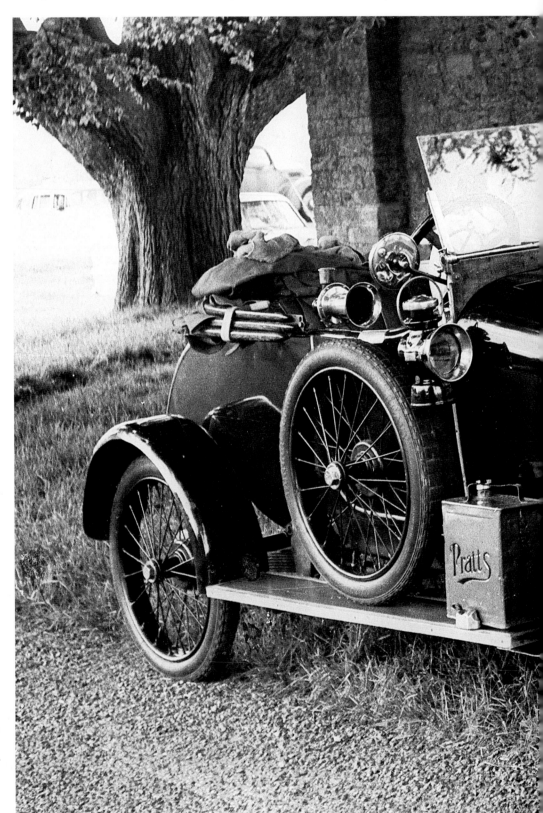

Like the Model T Ford, Le Zebre was priced low. Not only that, it was consistent—in losing wheels and breaking axles.

At right: A 1920 Le Zebre. That Le Zebres were nice-looking little cars can be seen here, but the issue at hand was keeping such a pleasant-seeming little car together and out of trouble: it had developed a reputation for breakdown that was exceptional even in that trial-and-error period of automotive engineering.

The first body style offered was a two-seater, and a four-seater was added to the line the following year. These early cars weighed 770 pounds (350 kg) and could attain 28 mph (45 kph).

These were followed by the similar Model C. This car developed six hp with a 47.9-cubic-inch (785-cc) four-cylinder engine. It was the smallest production four-cylinder car. It is said that the make's 'classic' period began in 1916.

The last Le Zebres, designed in 1919 for model year 1920, featured a 99-inch (2.5-meter) wheelbase, with both one-seater torpedo (narrow and rounded at both ends) and two-seater, deluxe, body styles. Power was provided by a 7.5-horsepower four-cylinder engine of 61 cubic inches (one liter) capacity, attached to a four-speed gearbox.

Le Zebre cars were cheap, and therefore, they sold despite their flaws. Even at that, the market dropped off, and the Le Zebre Company decided that size, not quality control, was the answer to their plunging profit margin. In 1920, the company dropped its small-car line and opted to build larger cars that apparently sold well enough to keep the business going until 1930.

CYCLE CARS AND GRAND EXPERIMENTS

Now that mankind had settled on the automobile as a suitable replacement for the horse, a plethora of design ideas poured forth from the automakers of the world. Some of these involved radically new bodywork; some involved drive train experiments that would, in some cases, dead-end in ignominy—while in others would propagate entire schools of theory. Some ideas combined new bodywork with new drive train concepts.

Still other automakers would develop the crudest methodology, combined with the utter minimum of materials, and sell the resultant product to a careless sector of the public that merely wanted to go fast at any cost—even if it meant their life.

In a sense, the 1920s offered what seemed to be a limitless perspective, with a standard of rather boxy—but at least substantial—automobiles, and outer fringes that ranged from the almost absurdly streamlined to the crudest and most inept attempts at automaking.

Running gear ranged from overhead camshaft designs and multi-speed transmissions to startling 'sliding ratio,' electronically-controlled transmissions coupled to monstrously large engines of low output. In short, it was a time of experimentation, and not all of the experiments succeeded.

1919–21 AV (Ward & Avey)

The AV was a very cheap 'cycle car' built by Ward & Avey (hence the phonetic 'AV'). It was strictly a single-seat vehicle, with spindly wire wheels and a minimal, arrowhead-shaped body. The engine was a JAP two-cylinder air-cooled unit that was mounted directly behind the driver—so close, in fact, that burns could result from its heat if you overstayed your welcome in the tiny cockpit.

This car weighed approximately 600 pounds (273 kg), and was very much like a projectile: indeed, the car's pointed nose may have been meant as a replacement for its practically nonexistent brakes—in a scrape, you could aim for the nearest tree, where the car would no doubt stick like an arrow—if it survived the impact.

The driver started the engine by pulling a chain, which activated a spring and rachet mechanism attached to the fly-wheel. In turn, the two-speed epicyclic transmission conveyed power to a chain that turned the rear axles. As such drive chains often broke, the driver was in some peril of being severely lacerated by same. The AV had no reverse.

With crude wire-and-bobbin steering (a staple of many such 'cycle cars') that was no better than most children fit to their home-made 'downhill racers,' this was a car that one aimed rather than drove. One foolhardy driver took his AV to 75 mph (120 kph) at Brooklands race track in England; the miracle is that he survived. The AV would have given Ralph Nader convulsions.

Opposite: A fearsome machine—in terms of safety rather than competition—the AV cycle-car. Its six-hp powerplant could propel it to 75 mph (120 kph)—far too fast for its flimsy design, which was better suited to pedal-power.

Note the pointed nose: the author wryly postulates that this was a back-up for the ridiculously inadequate braking system: if all else failed, the driver might have had to 'stick it in a tree.'

Worse yet, the machine shown here is a 1921 model—representing the upper end of AV Cycle-Car technology.

The AV was not alone in this slapdash school of design—there were cycle-cars that made the AV look like a veritable Rolls-Royce.

1920–27 Tamplin

This was another infamous cycle car. The Tamplin was a cut-rate machine designed to satisfy the urge to go fast—at any cost. The chassis and body were of monocoque construction, with an ash frame and waterproof fiberboard panels. The body configuration was an odd,

reverse wedge, with the base to the front. Gracing this (to be generous), were flat, plank-like fenders running along the car's belt-line.

The engine was an air-cooled JAP V-twin of 61-cubic-inch (one liter) capacity—a motorcycle engine, cranking out eight horsepower. This was attached to a Sturmey-Archer three-speed motorcycle gearbox, linked to a long, heavy chain that turned a large sprocket on the left rear wheel. As with most chain drives, there was always the danger of the chain's breaking under stress and lacerating the vehicle's occupants.

Tamplins at first were tandem two-

Above: *A 1922 Tamplin tandem cycle car.
Note the odd, reverse-wedge shape of the
body, and the split windshield—for leaning
into turns?*

*Not seen here is the monstrously long and
heavy drive chain, mounted on the vehicle's
left side.*

*Cycle-cars were ostensibly cheap
machines that allowed citizens of limited
means to have a motor car. Such cars as the
AV belonged under the ethical rubric,
'oppression of the lower classes.'*

seaters, but in 1922, this arrangement was
changed, and the cars were produced as
side-by-side two-seaters, with an all-
chain transmission. There was a kick-
starter in the driver's compartment.

Not a stable machine at all, this was a
car for those who had little money but an
overwhelming need to risk their lives.
The Tamplin had an 84-inch (two-meter)
wheelbase in its original tandem
configuration.

At the other end of the spectrum were
those cars that presented new horizons
in mechanical and aesthetic felicity. The
1920s would see considerable progress in
the designs of Bentley, Lancia, Hispano-
Suiza, Cord and other cars of mechanical
merit. Of course, there were those that
also sought the heights aggressively, and
failed.

1920 Crown Magnetic

Not quite as epochal an event in auto
history as it might have been (had it
worked), the Crown Magnetic's chief

drawing card was an unusual transmission that theoretically allowed the driver
an unlimited choice of gear ratios. However, theory once again collided with the
harsh realities of physical probability.

This car featured the Entz electromagnetic transmission, the rights to which
had been bought by Harry Crown, who
featured it in his Crown Magnetic cars.
An overcomplicated piece of machinery,
this transmission was so complex that its
manufacturers could only attempt to
explain its operation, and even in the
attempt, made it seem that the driver
had to *think* for the transmission, or it
would become confused.

The transmission, in fact, did become
confused, which is why the Crown Magnetic was a rare car even in its day. The
following is the manufacturer's *apologia*
for the workings of its electromagnetic
transmission.

'This system comprises two dynamo-
electric machines, located between the
prime mover and the driveshaft of the
vehicle, the first having its field mounted
upon the crankshaft of the gas engine in
the place of the usual flywheel and having its armature fixedly attached to the
driveshaft, and a second dynamo-elec-

tric machine having its armature also fixedly attached to the driveshaft and its field attached to the chassis-frame of the vehicle and consequently, stationary with respect to this armature.

'This relation of the machines must be firmly grasped in order to arrive at a proper understanding of the system and much confusion results from neglecting the fact that both elements of the first machine are movable and that the current generated in this machine is therefore a function of the difference in speed of two moving elements, one connected to the gas engine prime mover, and the other to the vehicle driveshaft.

'It will be evident from consideration of this point that an increase in speed of the driveshaft, so that the ratio of the speed of the prime mover to the speed of the driveshaft approaches unity, will cause a decrease in the amount of current generated in the first machine.'

The Crown Magnetic had a 142-inch (3.6-meter) wheelbase, and was powered by a 30 hp overhead-valve, six-cylinder engine of 415 cubic inches (6.8 liters). The transmission was meant to endow this car with a greater variety than any other transmission, so that one would be hard put to discern a definite number of 'gears.' Let's just say that it was an invention somewhat ahead of its time, depending too much on the arcane laws of electrodynamics to really make a 'go' of it.

The same year that his American car came out, Harry Crown invaded the British Isles and took over the Ensign Motor Car Company, a formerly respectable — if mediocre — automaker.

All cars produced thereafter by the company were known as Crown-Ensigns, and were *infected* with the Entz electromagnetic transmission. Thus diseased, Crown's ventures did not long endure the market.

Researchers have recently discovered a link between strong electromagnetic fields and the incidence of cancer in animals and humans — just one more reason that the Entz electromagnetic was probably well deserving of its demise.

Now for a car that was an oppression of the upper classes (see previous caption).

The Crown Magnetic was a well-knit car that had the world's most eccentric transmission. It was an electromagnetic apparatus that was so complex in its operation that the manufacturers could barely explain how it worked (essentially because it barely worked).

Below: A 1924 Crown Magnetic limousine. Not just the transmission was unusual — note the outboard leaf springs to the rear of the running board. The rear axle was sprung from the end of the leaf.

1920 Motobloc

Oddly innovative as the Crown Magnetic was, there were designs that sought an encompassing *conservatism*. Included in this genre were cars that sought to consolidate the drive train in ways that were not so radical as Edmund Rumpler's transaxle (see the chapter entitled 'They Might Have Been Great'), but economized on extant configurations by casting three-fourths of the drive train in a single block of iron.

Among these was the Motobloc—a compendium of seemingly good ideas

gone wrong. It was, to the casual observer, a nicely-finished but rather ordinary car of its time. Its claim to notoriety, of course, was its power train. In the early 1920s, the French had a penchant for simplifying drive trains that would seem, at first, admirable. But the ways in which they chose to simplify things were too often disastrous, as was witnessed by the one-piece engine, clutch housing and transmission casting of Le Zebre (see above).

Like Le Zebre, the Motobloc had its engine block, clutch housing and transmission cast in one piece. The manufacturers of the Motobloc escaped the prob-

lems of oil leakage from the engine to the transmission simply. They lubricated the engine, transmission and clutch with the same oil, so it didn't matter what leaked into what. However, the tradition of lubricating the engine and transmission with lubricants of different viscosity is based on thermodynamics.

Transmission fluid is of another consistency than engine oil because the lubricant requirements of meshing transmission gears, and the way in which the transmission lubricant must be distributed, are different than the requirements of an engine's crankshaft bearings, camshaft and valves, and the way in which the lubricant in the engine must be distributed.

Therefore, the ingenious one-oil-for-all scheme of the Motobloc served to cause frictional breakdown of main components. Not only that, but once the transmission, or the clutch, or an engine bearing failed, the entire unit had to be removed from the car so that the one part could be fixed.

This was, however, an automobile that performed remarkably vibration-free in all four forward gears. This was because the flywheel was incorporated into the engine design, and was located between the middle two of its four cylinders.

The incidence of flywheel explosion was much higher then than now. Such explosions are the result of centrifugal force interacting with metallurgic flaws in the flywheel, and advances in manufacturing processes have made this an increasingly rare event. Even so, automobiles still have a 'bell housing' that protects the driver and passenger from metal fragments should such an event occur.

In the then-likely event of an explosion, the Motobloc's positioning of the flywheel tended to shower bystanders with flywheel shrapnel, but the driver and passengers were relatively safe. However, the engine would be utterly destroyed by such an event—one reason manufacturers traditionally have opted for a flywheel outside of the cylinder bank proper. As to whether the super-smooth running of the car was worth the expense of repairing it, one would have to ask an owner.

The four-cylinder, 146-cubic-inch (2.4-liter) engine provided 12–15 hp, with an inlet-over-exhaust valve setup. With four forward speeds, the original Motobloc had a wheelbase of 118 inches (three meters). This car was produced throughout the 1920s.

1920–21 Duplex

Cars of the 1920s generally had engines of four, six or eight cylinders, with the occasional two-cylinder hangover in examples of the cycle-car, and the occasional V-12 in the case of upscale luxury and performance cars. Two common aspects of these engines have become traditions that hold true today: each cylinder tended to have its own spark plug, and each was equipped with both inlet and exhaust valves.

Opposite: *A rear view of a Motobloc touring car, as outfitted for the rigors of the Tour du Monde.*

Motobloc main drivetrain components were interconnected, allowing oil and particles from the transmission to invade the crankcase—promoting early main bearing failure, among other breakdowns.

Also, with its flywheel mounted mid-engine, disaster was always close at hand for the Motobloc (see text).

Above: *A 1920 Duplex roadster. Simple-looking as it was, its egregiously inefficient power plant insured that Duplex cars would not long grace the thoroughfares of the world.*

Cylinders shared spark plugs, yet divided the chores of intake and exhaust according to which one had which valve!

Below: *A Reese Aero-car. At 150 pounds (68 kg), it was probably the lightest of the propeller-driven cars. As with others of its genre, it was a rolling menace.*

Given the above, the Duplex was a car of considerable technical interest—which words, when appearing in a book like this, are a 'red flag.' The Duplex had a wheelbase of 106 inches (2.6 meters), and its engine had eight cylinders arranged in pairs. The cylinder head was cast in such a way that each pair of cylinders shared a sparkplug. Also, one cylinder of each pair had the inlet valve and the other contained the outlet valve.

This odd little engine had 91.5 cubic inches (1.5 liters) and was claimed to produce 10 horsepower. It failed to generate the excitement that it might have had it proven to be efficient, and the Duplex was manufactured only in 1920 and 1921.

Then again, some designs were too careless in their rush toward what was felt to be an 'optimum' condition, and, as with Edmund Rumpler's Tropfen-Autos (see the chapter entitled 'They Might Have Been Great'), the automobile's developmental links with other modes of transportation sometimes burst through the surface of a designer's inspiration in uncomfortably—and unsuccessfully—overt ways.

1921–25 Scott Sociable

This was a cycle-car that was perhaps more 'cycle' than 'car,' and whose links to the motorcycle severely compromised its design. It was intended to be a touch more comfortable than a motorcycle and sidecar. A three-wheel automobile with an offset wheel arrangement, this little vehicle weighed 500 pounds (227 kg) and was powered by a five horsepower, two-stroke powerplant. It got phenomenal gas mileage, but, riding the narrow line between being a motorcycle and/or being a car, the little machine was eccentrically balanced, not recommended for higher speeds or sudden turns.

It had some of the characteristics of a motorcycle-and-sidecar arrangement, but without the flexibility, and could be extraordinarily treacherous to drive. The Scott Sociable had a wheelbase of 61 inches (1.6 meters).

Just as the Scott Sociable was a bit too close to the line between the automobile and the motorcycle, partaking of the disadvantages of either design, so too, other inspirations partook of onerous aspects of their prime integer without real advantages.

For instance, the MacDuff Aeropinion/Pneumoslito (see the previous text on same) borrowed the propulsion mechanism of the airplane, yet remained a vehicle utterly unsuited for flight. Even so, this line of development saw further permutations through the years.

1922 Reese Aero-car

While some manufacturers, such as Prado Motors of New York City, were interested in adapting aircraft engines to conventional automotive power trains, the makers of the Reese Aero-Car opted to adapt the land-going automobile to aircraft propulsion—as did the earlier designers of the MacDuff Aeropinion/Pneumonslito.

The Aero-car was equipped with a propeller, and needed no other drive train. However, while it succeeded as a vehicle that would carry passengers and made progress at a good rate over the ground, it was also a hazard to bystanders due to its whirling propeller, and made an atrocious amount of noise.

1926 McLaughlin Maine-mobile

The prop-driven car as a concept was given yet more life by the McLaughlin Maine-mobile, which was a propeller-driven automobile that was not only amphibious, but also convertible into a sled. Its 72-horsepower engine was claimed, by McLaughlin himself, to provide automotive speed of up to 106 mph (170 kph). On the water, this predecessor of today's 'swamp buggies' could speed along at 35 mph (56.3 kph or 30 knots), and on the snow, it could manage a similar blistering pace.

The problem here was much the same as that with the Reese Aero-car and the MacDuff Aeropinion/Pneumoslito: the whirling propeller could wreak havoc with its surroundings if an accident occurred, and made an excruciating amount of noise.

Not only that, but wheeled, land-going, vehicles are far better controlled if the power transmission is through the wheels: one can exert control of motion not just through braking, but also through gear selection, which helps to modulate not only the amount of drag on the vehicle's inertial mass, but also the relative amount of grip the wheels have by intelligent use of throttle, brake and gearshift.

In the case of the Maine-mobile, the Aero-car and the Pneumoslito, the vehicle in its landgoing configuration was essentially free-wheeling except when the brakes were applied. The driver had not as much control as was desirable over a vehicle that thrashed the air with a potentially lethal propeller while barrelling along at 106 mph (170 kph).

Nor was this the end of attempts to revolutionize the running gear of the automobile. Other attempts focused on the engine—in some cases, with stunning effect, as in the Duesenberg and the Bugatti. Still others attempted to meld greater simplicity to extant technology, and produced machines that had subtle, yet bizarre, aspects.

1920 Hungerford Rocket

Daniel, Floyd and William Hungerford, the proprietors of the 'Hungerford Brothers Automobile and Aeroplane

Repairing and Building' shop in Elmira, New York, were self-taught aeronautical engineers. They had invented two airplane engines themselves, and—since Elmira was then the glider plane capital of the world—were in an element that could easily support their activities.

The experiments of such rocketry enthusiasts as Fritz von Opel and Max Valier, and the advent of the futuristic 'Buck Rogers' comic strip, inspired Daniel and Floyd Hungerford to expand their creative horizons to rocket power

(brother William was not interested in such).

Von Opel, for instance, had designed and built a rocket car called the German Opel RAK 11, in 1928. It was a torpedo-style car, powered by 24 small rockets using powdered explosive as a fuel. The RAK 11 attained speeds in excess of 90 mph (144 kph). Unfortunately, both the car and its inventor died in a fiery crash.

Also in 1928, Max Valier built a rocket sled and a rocket car—both propelled by liquified oxygen, a dangerously unstable substance. Valier died when his car exploded during a test run in 1930. Von Opel and Valier were to be linked with the Hungerfords in being the most widely publicized of the early rocket-car experimenters.

In 1929, the comic strip 'Buck Rogers' burst upon the American scene, and became an immediate success with its projections as to what the future might be. Central to the twenty-fifth century lifestyle it projected was the rocket engine, which not only powered space craft, but land vehicles as well.

Daniel and Floyd Hungerford made careful studies of rocket-powered space flight, and determined that it could,

Below: *The McLaughlin Maine-Mobile, one of the more substantial-looking propeller cars. The* Bangor Daily Commercial *likened its bulbous contours to 'a small war tank.'*

It was adaptable to run on land, water or snow, and its top speed was 106 mph (170 kph): it would have been a lethal weapon at just one-third that speed.

Overleaf: *A Scott Sociable, in a scenario that sends chills down the spine. As they were ready for an outing in this monstrous little car that was designed* minus *a left front wheel, one only wonders if this family survived—and whether the designer of this car could sleep at night.*

Like a phantom from a Social Darwinist's most twisted fantasies, this cheap little Cycle-car would have well suited a plot to eliminate the less financially fortunate. ('Survival of the fittest,' indeed.)

At top, above: *Rocketeer-cum-automaker Daniel Hungerford in the driver's seat of the original version of the Hungerford Rocket Car—also known as Shirley Lois, Moon Girl, for Daniel's eight-year-old daughter.*

The Hungerfords' ultimate dream is here encoded for all to see, on the body panelling just behind Daniel's head.

The Shirley Lois, Moon Girl was, in a sense, a rocket 'going incognito' as a car—as is evidenced by the New York State vehicle registration card shown above.

This was the first, and probably the only, rocket-powered vehicle ever licensed to operate on public thoroughfares.

indeed, be accomplished. They decided, however, to make their first large-scale rocket project a land vehicle.

They modified a 1921 Chevrolet chassis, leaving the original drive train in place for everyday travel. At the rear of the car, they mounted a single rocket motor that ran on a combination of gasoline and forced air. To feed fuel to the rocket motor, a pump was devised to run off the vehicle's driveshaft.

To run the car in rocket mode, the car had to be sitting still. Then, the driver pulled a lever that brought certain alterations in the drive train into play, causing—among other things—the clutch to become inactive, and it was said that the driver changed gears without using the clutch!

The car was then accelerated under conventional power, and when the driver shifted into high gear, a valve opened to feed gasoline to the rocket motor, ignition for which was supplied by a spark plug controlled by a driver-operated switch. The switch was thrown for rocket power when the car had attained 50 mph (80 kph).

The car's first run was made, strictly on conventional power, on 2 November 1929, when Daniel and Floyd Hungerford took it for a tour of Elmira, to the amazement of local residents.

It was an astonishing-looking car, with a body shaped like the teardrop-like Buck Rogers spaceships. Its designated name was also an optimistic dedication to Daniel's eight-year-old daughter: *Shirley Lois, Moon Girl.* Five rocket nozzles

bristled at the rear of the car—though only one was real, while the other four were for effect.

The carbody was composed of linoleum and cardboard panels, to give the driver the option of kicking through the side of the car for quick escape if trouble arose. Isinglass—a clear gelatin—was used for the curving front windows, and regular glass was used for the square portholes along the sides.

The rocket motor was built of stovepipe iron, with combustion chambers that were lined at first with porcelain, which tended to crack in the tremendous heat of operation. Carborundum was later substituted as a combustion-chamber lining.

The Chevrolet's standard rear-wheel brakes were left intact, but an ingenious system of service and emergency brakes was combined with a series of cables and pulleys to provide extra braking power at speed.

Portable seats provided accomodation for the driver and one passenger. The *Shirley Lois, Moon Girl*'s appearance underwent numerous changes as the years rolled on, but the words 'Hungerford Rockets, Solar & Interstellar, Elmira, NY' remained a constant rear panel decoration. Its wheelbase was 102 inches (2.6 meters), with a treadwidth of 64 inches (162 cm) and an overall length of 184 inches (4.7 meters).

The Hungerfords tried time and again to get publicity—which might have meant research money—for their ongoing project. At one point Daniel Hungerford wrote to the makers of Cocomalt (a chocolate beverage mix), who sponsored a Buck Rogers radio program, circa 1932. Daniel pled to have his letter, describing the rocket car, read after the regular broadcast. The letter was in fact read over the air, but without much effect. Also, 'Buck Rogers' himself answered Daniel Hungerford with a personally-signed letter that was mailed, one presumes, from the twenty-fifth century!

In rocket mode, the *Shirley Lois, Moon Girl* attained 70 mph (112 kph) (though its gas mileage dropped to two mpg [3.2 kpg]). Trailing a 20-foot (six-meter) rocket flame, the car was spectacular in operation. Therefore, the Hungerford brothers took their creation on tour to fairgrounds and airports in the New York-Pennsylvania area. This activity never failed to attract a crowd, but again, serious support for Hungerford endeavors was not forthcoming.

While Daniel did some lecturing at Elmira College and Cornell University in the mid-1930s, not much help was generated in that venue, either. The brothers tried to get permission to display their rocket car at Chicago's 'A Century of Progress' exhibition in 1933, and failed. Likewise, a request to display the vehicle at the 1939 New York World's Fair was rejected.

Had the Hungerfords been able to generate support, their long-range plans included a Moon rocket, and an advanced electromagnetic propulsion system. The Hungerford brothers also invented a rocket-powered soldering iron, which applied rocket principles to heat the solder and make it flow fast; and a rocket lawn mower, the exact nature of which has been lost to posterity.

The last large-scale exhibition of the *Shirely Lois, Moon Girl* was on 29 July 1934, at Colusey's Airport in Coudersport, Pennsylvania. The grand vision was taking a toll on the Hungerfords. By the end of the 1930s, Daniel's marriage failed, and he and Floyd then shared a house. They slowly became hermits—

lauded by some as geniuses, and denounced by others as quacks.

The *Shirley Lois, Moon Girl* was the only rocket-powered car ever licensed for use on a public thoroughfare. Its State of New York Department of Motor Vehicles registration card read: 'Make of Vehicle—Chevrolet; Type—Rocket Car.'

Certainly, the *Shirley Lois, Moon Girl* was not a vehicle one could tailgate lightly. Likewise, those trapped behind it in traffic had some cause for fear, with those rocket nozzles just a few feet from their car's windshield.

The car is currently intact, located somewhere in Albany, New York—not far from its home town. It's probably just as well that it didn't catch on. Imagine Hungerford Rockets blasting along country lanes and highways by the hundreds: pedestrians would have to wear flame-retardant suits, and all car windows would have to be rolled up as a *Shirley Lois, Moon Girl* duplicate passed by with a belch of flame. Imagine the insurance suits for paint blisters!

Below: *Daniel Hungerford posing at the rear of a 1930s incarnation of the* Shirley Lois, Moon Girl.

The only functioning rocket nozzle shown here is the one in the center. The larger, surrounding tubes were merely the products of wishful thinking.

The Hungerford Rocket Car could attain 70 mph (112 kph), on a gasoline/forced air mixture. Mileage was low, at two mpg.

As can be seen from these photos, the vehicle's exterior sheathing underwent changes through the years. Also, note that the body-panel message had become less proclamatory, and more evocative.

STREAMLINERS
AND
FLYING CARS

The 1930s were a time of transition. The automobile was now undoubtedly the vehicle of the century, and would do as much to define and change the life of the average person in the Western World as had World War I. With this increasing importance, the automobile itself was undergoing rapid change. The 1930s began with flaring fenders, wide, vertical grilles and running boards. By the end of the decade, fenders began to merge integrally into the bodies of most cars, and grilles began to narrow, while windshields began to attain a degree of backward slope that had been the hallmark of the most sporting Bentley and the most elegant Bugatti.

After World War II, the march of change not only continued, but accelerated, and the streamlining experiments of the 1930s saw the advent of such completely faired-in bodies as the Crosley and the fabulous, but ill-fated, Tucker car.

These developments were, of course, not without their pitfalls. Also, the long-hood look was not to be completely effaced until the late 1940s—which brings us to focus on another aspect of auto development in the 1930s. This was the era of really large, complex engines, with straight-eights, V-12s and even V-16s tucked away under those long engine bonnets.

In turn, this brought about the question of balancing the car's weight, as well as its overall design. At least one auto-maker had a truly *straightforward* answer to this question.

1934 Voisin

Normally a maker of elegant and respectable autos, Gabriel Voisin was also known to also have his eccentricities. He had been a pioneer aeronaut before he turned to the manufacturing of automobiles. For some reason, Voisin became a steadfast adherent of sleeve valve-type engines, which were generally thought of as low-revving and relatively low-power engines. Voisin did have a knack, however, and in 1927, an 489-cubic-inch (eight-liter) Voisin set a world record by maintaining 128 mph (206 kph) for an hour.

At least one Voisin engine, a V-12, anticipated the usual kinds of problems that were endemic to sleeve-valve designs—namely, the valves tended to pop out when the going got really rough. This V-12 had numerous safeguards built in especially to keep the valves from falling into the engine oil sump, if severe difficulties arose.

The crowning eccentricity of Voisin's

Below: A 1934 Voisin. The admirable felicity of line seen here concealed an in-line 12-cylinder engine, composed of two blocks of six cylinders each. Front-seat passengers could practically pat the engine for good luck if they so chose.

The oval windows on top were part of a sliding sun roof which is shown in the open position here. Passengers needed the ventilation, as extreme engine proximity meant lots of heat.

automotive efforts was unveiled in 1934. This car had an in-line 12-cylinder engine, arranged in two separate blocks of six cylinders. It is surmised that this extremely long powerplant arrangement was Voisin's way of bringing the engine's center of gravity closer to the geometrical center of the car.

The engine extended rearward so far that part of it came between the driver and the front-seat passenger. But for its extended firewall, this was one car that would let you pat the engine for luck, if you were so inclined.

Engine heat flooded the car's cockpit from the proximity of the powerplant, and the very eccentricity of the engine's position was an item of discomfiture for other than sheer lovers of machinery. This Voisin was a large car, with a wheelbase of approximately 132 inches (3.4 meters).

A passing reference here should be made to an even more radical approach to auto design: that of America's R Buckminster Fuller, whose Dymaxion Car of 1933 was a three-wheeled, rear-engine, V-8-powered, van-like vehicle that resembled a sow bug with its beetling

profile and integrated wheel wells.

The Dymaxion car claimed great advantages, including the ability to make a 360-degree turn within its own wheelbase, effected by the single, rearward, directional wheel.

While its career ended with a tragic accident, the Dymaxion still has its share of ferocious adherents. Whether it was a good or bad car, however, the Dymaxion Car (of which there were three variants) announced a new era of experimentation in which Edmund Rumpler's Tropfen-Auto (see the chapter entitled 'They Might Have Been Great') would have been at home.

1934–37 Chrysler Airflow

Chrysler cars in the late 1920s and early 1930s were paradigms of excellent design, spearheaded by the luxurious Imperial, which featured bodywork by LeBaron and DeDietrich, and were emulated by designers all over the world.

Above: *A DeSoto Airflow of the 1934 model year. The DeSoto was Chrysler's 'companion line,' and shared Chrysler's stylistic woes.*

Overleaf: *A bevy of 1934 Chrysler Airflows on display. Seen from this view only, the front-end design of the car to the right of the photo almost makes sense, although the blunted profile, enormously sad-looking headlights and grillework resembled the face of an insect.*

An industrial-style windshield did not help, and the sweeping lines of the car flowed together in such a way as to emphasize that its revolting aspect had actually been planned, making a bad impression immeasurably worse.

While the idea of faired-in fenders did, in fact, catch on, it is a relief that the Airflow design in particular did not catch on. A highway full of these would have resembled an aphid-infested branch.

Above: *A 1937 Chrysler Airflow, which repre-sented the last year in production of what was then the ugliest of cars. The protruding snout of this car was an attempt to redeem the design enough to sell a few more to die-hard Chrysler lovers. Actually, the car rode well, and was comfortable—but its appear-ance caused sufficient gloom to more than overcome these positive aspects.*

However, the voice of 'progress' was insistently making itself heard within the halls of the Chrysler Corporation.

Citing the steady advances in aircraft design that had been made through the years, Chrysler engineer Carl Breer convinced his peers and superiors to follow up their established success with a ground-breaking car that would exploit the use of wind tunnel technology. One wonders if Breer had somehow met Edmund Rumpler (see the chapter entitled 'They Might Have Been Great').

After much brainstorming, Breer and associates developed a car that had semi-unitary construction, and was to be more drag-efficient than any American auto had ever been before.

What was hoped to be a shining moment of glory came in 1934, when Breer's brainchild was unveiled as the Chrysler Airflow and its companion line,

the DeSoto Airflow. Mechanically not a bad car, it was a horrendous-*looking* thing, with a blunt, downward-sloping nose; an ungainly, top-heavy look; and a windshield that appeared to have been borrowed from an industrial conveyance of some kind.

Though it was dimensionally much like an average mid-sized car of the period, the public quite understandably shied away from this monstrosity. While the design has often enough been touted as 'ahead of its time,' it was misbegotten—a triumph of engineering over style and appeal. True, the Airflow was roomy and comfortable to drive, but the public could not overcome their revulsion.

A total sales disaster, the Airflow design had been a major corporate mistake for Chrysler. Sheerly for the sake of 'keeping a stiff upper lip,' Chrysler Corporation continued production of the

DeSoto Airflow until 1936, while that of the marginally better-selling Chrysler Airflow was dragged on to 1937.

(The company, in desperation, sold an attachable nose for retrofitting on Airflow models. This nose included grillwork and a hood, and helped to lessen the Airflow's buglike 'man from Mars' front end look.)

Europe, at the same time, saw streamlining of an equally radical nature burst upon the scene under the guidance of Hans Ledwinka. Perhaps it was because Ledwinka and company took the notion of streamlining so seriously that they quite fearlessly armed some of their cars with huge dorsal fins, adding to the 'species from another element' mystique of their autos.

1934–38 Tatra Model 77

Not only Ledwinka, but Paul Jaray also was interested in streamlined automobiles. Jaray had worked as a Zeppelin designer, and believed in wind tunnel testing. He sought to imbue his designs with as much aerodynamic sophistication as possible. Jaray's cars began to resemble Futurist sculpture, with their appearance of having been formed by 'lines of force.' The bodies tended to be tall and narrow, with ducktail curves in evidence throughout. While fascinating, when built full-scale, they tended to be more startling or shocking than actually attractive.

Ledwinka, on the other hand, was a more conventional aesthete, and produced designs that appeared more like cars, and less like rolling sculpture. Ledwinka favored a laterally flattened, fastback rearend, with a single vertical fin, or 'vertical stabilizer' *a la* the conventional airplane. Both of these men found their 'angel' in the auto manufacturer Tatra of Czechoslovakia.

In fact, Ledwinka had worked for Tatra since the firm's inception, and was unquestionably inspired by his old boss, Edmund Rumpler (see the chapter entitled 'They Might Have Been Great'). Proof of this is that the prototype of the Tatra Model 77 had its driving-station centrally

Below: A 1934 Tatra Model 77. Its rear-mounted V-8 made it a fast and very dangerous car to drive, as it was notoriously unstable at speed.

Note the air scoops for the engine, and the budding rear stabilizer fin, which would become more prominent in later Tatras.

The front end resembles a refined version of the Chrysler and DeSoto Airflow cars just previously discussed. This is no surprise, as Airflows, as well as Model 77s, were designed with extant wind-tunnel technology.

located *a la* the Tropfen-Autos (please see the text on these cars) of the 1920s, but dropped the design as impractical for production.

Ledwinka's Tatras had a vogue among well-to-do artistic people who delighted in the cars' outrageous dorsal fins and slippery, 'non-bourgeois' profile. There was also an element of daring to drive a Tatra Model 77. It seemed that Tatra had not worked out the ergonomics of its design. With tubular chassis, monocoque bodies and rear-mounted, air-cooled V-8 engines, the Tatras had top speeds of approximately 90 mph (144 kph), but were highly unstable machines, and had severe control problems over 50 mph (80 kph).

In a car whose major selling points were sporty styling and high performance, this was the worst of possible problems. Even so, the original, 183-cubic-inch (three-liter), 60-hp engine was replaced with a 207-cubic-inch (3.4-liter) 72-hp engine. The car's fatal accident rate was such that the German Army forbade its officers to drive Tatras because of this trait.

Back on the American side of the Atlantic, a private carbuilder was readying his own streamlined offering.

1938 Phantom Corsair

The Phantom Corsair, based on a Cord automobile chassis, was more an outright failure of styling than of design. The Cord Company had been responsible for some very good-looking automobiles.

This was partly because Cord chassis, with their high-performance engines and exotic front-wheel-drive configuration, were naturals for any designer with a yen for sleekness and exclusivity. Among the designers Cord cooperated with were Gordon Buehrig and Carl Van Ranst, who turned out notable designs for the L-29, the 810 and the 812 Berline.

However, there were those designers who had dreams of beauty and elegance but were unable to realize them—either through their own love of idiosyncracy, or through lack of talent. Perhaps the worst designs were those perpetrated by the designer with zeal but unclear purpose. In other words, a misguided designer without zeal is not likely to present a forceful design: the travesty he presents to the public will not likely be one that impresses itself on the memory.

Below: *A late-1930s Tatra, exhibiting much the same body design as the car seen on Page 49. Note the aircraft-inspired 'vertical stabilizer' on the rear of its body.*

This same basic design was retained for years after the initial design of the 77, with minor changes here and there.

Opposite: *A Tatra on a European boulevard. Hans Ledwinka's sleek design was, all too often, a fatal lure for the foolhardy.*

Above: *A frontal view of the Phantom Corsair, an example of the 'zealous but misguided' school of design. This car was created for Hollywood by Rust Heinz, an otherwise capable designer.*

He charged the studio moguls $25,000 for the privilege of giving studio crews an object they could name 'The Flying Wombat.'

In 1938, $25,000 was enough to induce almost anyone to give birth to a 'wombat' or two. Note the blunt snout of this car and the 'flaring-nostril' louvers—not to mention the conflicting headlight/turn signal design.

However, the misguided but *zealous* designer is likely leave his attention-getting imprint on his work, and is likely to present something *unforgettably* hideous, or *unforgettably* ludicrous.

This latter was the case with Rust Heinz's design for the Cord 810 chassis. The design was obviously supposed to be a sleek, futuristic bombshell of a car, powered by a high-performance Lycoming straight-eight engine. It was, in a way, ahead of its time, with completely faired-in fenders, and a low silhouette. However, its proportions were all wrong, and the fender sides dropped straight down from the windows like the sandguards on British Crusader tanks of the period—an effect that was only emphasized by the full skirts on the front and rear wheels.

The headlights were 'cat's eyes,' vertical-slit units, set in sockets that were molded bulbs of metal set down into the sloping curve of the tub-like front end.

They very strongly resembled the eyes of a semi-submerged hippopotamus, and also evoked a sense of bemused loneliness. Set below and to the outside of these, on the outer curve of the fender line, were foglights presented in a manner that was out of keeping, even with the bad standard set by the rest of the car.

These foglights were set behind teardrop-shaped glass protectors that sloped down at the corners. The lights themselves were near-headlight-size bulbs, surrounded by chromed flashing, giving the foglights the appearance of eyes—very sad, and unsettlingly alien-looking eyes. Since the foglight units appeared to be larger than the headlight units, this front end had the additional novelty of looking like it was upside-down.

Set between the lights, in a vertical, truncated 'V,' was a double row of louvers that decreased in extent as they descended the bulbous nose of the car, and were flared in such a way as to suggest fierceness, or rage, as in an African mask, or the nostrils of a horse or a cow, in sextuplicate.

It should be borne in mind that designers seek to evoke a particular emotion with their designs. It can be seen, however, that the Phantom Corsair front end presented a number of emotions, none of which was coherent in this jumble of stylistic sensations.

As a whole, the car looked fat, and behind the absurd front end, the sides ran back in unbroken plainness, without so much as a door handle to the seamless monotony.

The cockpit was very low, in keeping with the generally low profile of the car. However, with the unrelieved flatness of its sides, which made the car look massive, this also contributed to the generally impression of a mechanical hippopotamus, which leads this author to conjecture that Rust Heinz might have been viewing a Tarzan movie before he launched into designing this car.

Be that as it may, a limited production run was planned, but never realized. This may be due to the car's reception in its big chance at a public-relations coup, which came when the car was featured in the 1938 Selznick International Films motion picture *The Young at Heart*, starring Douglas Fairbanks Jr and Janet Gaynor. The Phantom Corsair emerged from this venture with a new, popular moniker—the 'Flying Wombat,' which was given it by the film crew.

If nothing else, this very decisively quashed Rust Heinz' hopes for marketing his design. While the idea—ie, a car with a low profile and faired-in fenders and seamless, futuristic styling—was a good one, its realization, in this case, was definitely not.

The last word in futuristic design lay not with body styling, however, but with a deeper plunge into the usages of the wind tunnel than any of the streamlined cars. Flying cars broke the boundary between *seeming* to fly along in one's automobile, and *literally* flying in same.

The concept of a flying car or a roadable airplane has been with us since the advent of both forms of transportation. This is only natural, as both began serious development at the turn of the century, with Daimler, Benz and Ford making breakthroughs in automobile

Below: *The silhouette of the Phantom Corsair. The motoring public of the late 1930s often accused automakers of shrinking the vertical dimensions of car windows to a dangerous and uncomfortable degree. In Heinz's design, as seen here, the windows have almost disappeared.*

This car resembles an elongated camel's head, complete with a drooping lip at the front end.

It was built on a Cord 810 chassis, complete with a potent Lycoming straight-eight engine, and was designed to be a glimpse of what a car could be. Note the full skirts on the wheel wells. In a turn, you'd either lose or damage the front skirts.

Flying auto is this strange vehicle, perfected by famous flyer Waldo Waterman. A car on the highways, it adds wings at its hangar and smoothly takes to the skyways. Its power plant is a 6-cylinder Studebaker Dictator engine which operates on ordinary filling station gas.

Above: *A Studebaker advertisement propounding the Waterman Aerobile to the public. Note this vehicle's tricycle running gear.*

As a backer of the project, Studebaker's hopes were so high that, as is pictured here, they envisioned Aerobiles blending into the highway environment well enough to get 'moving violation' tickets just like every other car.

The Aerobile here is shown minus its detachable wings.

design; and the Wright Brothers, Otto Lilienthal and Samuel Langley making breakthroughs in heavier-than-air flight design. The most notable inventor of *flightless*, landgoing airplanes, of course, was Edmund Rumpler (see the chapter entitled 'They Might Have Been Great').

Both the automobile and the airplane were perceived as symbols of progress, and both were emblematic of power, speed and a Nietzschean freedom from the constraints of the Earth — specifically, all previous forms of overland travel.

Even that well-known pioneer of airplane design, Glenn Curtiss, produced a design for a three-seat flying car for the Pan-American Aeronautic Exposition of 1917. This hybrid craft performed its intended functions, but did so poorly, and Curtiss turned his attentions fully to aircraft design.

1937 Waterman Aerobile (or Arrowbile)

The next notable attempt to create a flying car was Waldo Waterman's Aerobile of 1937. It wasn't a bad-looking machine, and the wings came off easily for road use. Unfortunately, the Aerobile was bred for two separate environments, and the conflicts inherent in such a hybridization showed in its performance.

As an airplane, it had to carry the extra weight of automobile running gear — transmission, differential and four

wheels — plus it had a body with a drag coefficient such that it would stay on the ground when it was meant to be a car.

As an automobile, it sported the propeller shaft mechanism of an airplane, and had a body that was 'slippery' enough for flying, but not necessarily designed for *stability* on the ground, where different aerodynamic requirements applied. Additionally, its automotive running gear was necessarily minimal enough to save weight for the airplane mode.

Even so, the Studebaker Company liked the idea well enough to contemplate selling the Aerobile through their dealer network, and a version of the Aerobile was built with a Studebaker six-cylinder powerplant.

Had the deal with Studebaker gone through, all subsequent Aerobiles would have sported Studebaker sixes instead of the design's original Franklin horizontally-opposed six. The hybrid's too-narrow capabilities in either of its intended arenas of operation caused Studebaker to dismiss the plan, eventually.

1939 Pitcairn PA-36 Whirlwing

Close on the heels of the Aerobile's initial development was the Pitcairn PA-36 Whirlwing, which was designed by Juan de la Cierva in 1939.

The Pitcairn PA-36 approached the 'flying car' concept by way of the then-popular autogyro. The basic autogyro was like an ordinary prop-driven airplane in most respects, but with a helicopter rotor instead of forward wings. This aspect gave the autogyro — and its design offspring, the Pitcairn PA-36 flying car — the ability to land and take off in a limited space.

Even with this helicopter-like ability, the Pitcairn PA-36 lacked sufficient practicality, due to the limitations of its hybrid design, which were similar to those from which the Waterman Aerobile suffered.

However, the flying car had a resurgence in the era of post-World War II optimism. To the average person, the end of that war was like emerging from under a huge black cloud, and suddenly the vista was endless, promising limitless possibilities. The world was abuzz with new solutions to old problems, and among the many wonders held up was the bright prospect of 'an aircraft in every garage.'

1946 Spratt Controllable Wing Car/Skycar

Designed by George Spratt, the Spratt Controllable Wing Car featured a pusher-type propeller, and had a flexible wing mounted on a swivel behind its two-passenger cab. Early marketing efforts for this flying car failed, so Spratt teamed up with William Stout and his Stout Aircraft Company. They then remarketed the Spratt Controllable Wing Car as the Sky-car—again, without success.

As noted in the case of the Waterman Aerobile, flying cars were compromise designs, and hence had distinct disadvantages when compared to either airplanes or cars. Also, the sudden post-war abundance of military-surplus light aircraft made buying a *real* airplane cheaper—for those who wanted to fly—than buying a brand-new vehicle that cost more and had compromised performance characteristics.

1947 Hervey Travelplane

Still, plucky flying-car makers continued on. In 1947, the Hervey Travelplane—designed by George Hervey of Roscoe,

California—was made available for purchase. This unique design had a single tail boom that passed through the shaft of its pusher-type propeller.

The Hervey Travelplane was powered by a 200-hp Ranger engine that allowed four hours of flying time at 125 mph (200 kph). This design had a 192-inch (4.8-meter) carbody and a 35-foot (10.5-meter) wingspan.

The Hervey Travelplane came complete with a trailer for stowing the detachable wings.

1947 Whitaker-Zuck Planemobile

Also offered in 1947, the Whitaker-Zuck Planemobile needed no trailer for its wings. This flying car had a 228-inch (5.8-meter) carbody, and a wingspan of 32.5 feet (9.9 meters). The wings folded

Below: *Looking much like a helicopter, this prototype of the Spratt Controllable Wing Car had room for two passengers in its cab. Neither George Spratt, nor his eventual partner, William Stout, could make the vehicle a success—even when they gave it the catchy name of 'Skycar.'*

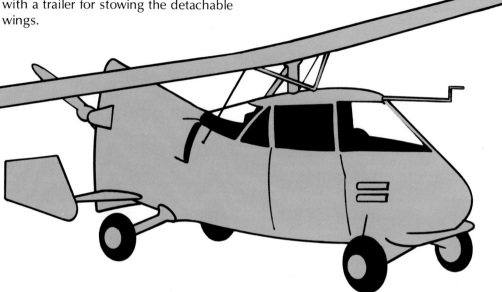

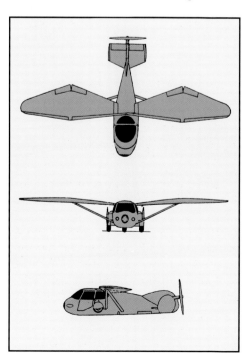

At far left: *Three views of the Hervey Travelplane. Note the pusher-type propeller, the central hub of which supports the extended tail boom.*

While such flying cars seemed the ultimate convenience at first glance, it became more apparent with each effort that the best approach to land/air travel is to design vehicles dedicated to each environment.

At left: *Views of the Whitaker-Zuck Planemobile. If it looks a beetle with wings extended, the resemblance increased when the wings were folded across the top for highway travel. All the planemobile lacked for a full similitude were elytra.*

The Taylor Aerocar (opposite) was one of several flying cars that had detachable wings and tail. In this case, a trailer was provided on which to carry them.

In later years, Moulton Taylor faired the wheels into the body, so that the body resembled one of those egg-shaped Japanese cars of the 1960s.

across the back of the car for highway use, rather like an insect. Further the wings were broader at the base, as is the case with beetles.

As to the originality of this design— Vladimir Tatlin, the famous early-twentieth-century Russian sculptor, invented an insect-like glider that now hangs in a Soviet museum. Whether Tatlin inspired the Planemobile, we cannot positively say.

1949 Taylor Aerocar

Moulton Taylor's Taylor Aerocar appeared in 1949. This V-tailed flying machine converted relatively easily for road use, and had a trailer for its folded wings.

It had shopping-cart-like wheels that protruded from its sides.

1946–52 Fulton Airphibian

Perhaps the most ingenious of all the flying cars was the Fulton FA-3 Airphibian, whose name was a play on the word 'amphibian.'

The Airphibian was a two-place airplane until it landed. At that point, the operator could release a few catches and simply drive the forward part of the fuselage away, sans wings and aeronautic trappings.

The Fulton Airphibian (below) looked much like a conventional small plane until it landed and drove away from its wings and fuselage, like a lizard losing its tail.

Indeed, it was intended to grant drivers freedom from the confines of the ground. Unfortunately, the Airphibian was itself confined by being too much a hybrid.

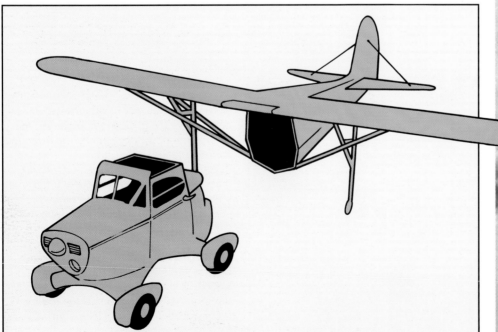

When Consolidated Vultee/Convair bought the Hall Flying Car idea, they transformed it into the four-wheel ConVairCar (above).

The ConVairCar used a wholly detachable flying apparatus, including a separate powerplant, for their revised flying car. Also see the caption on Page 59.

Though there was to be at least one more flying car attempt, this was the project that really spelled the end for flying cars in the mass marketplace (see text).

1945–46 Hall Flying Car/ ConVairCar

The most practical of flying cars was invented by Theodore 'Ted' Hall, an engineer at Consolidated Vultee Aircraft (now known as Convair) in San Diego. Hall had been caught up in a vision of personalized flying cars for the masses. He quit his job at Consolidated Vultee in 1945 to work on a design.

Hall soon had a partner, his former fellow worker at Consolidated Vultee, Tom Thompson. The flying car they made had a body of lightweight aluminum on a tubular steel framework, with a 90-hp Franklin engine for flying, and a four-cylinder, 26.5-hp Crosley engine for driving on the road.

The vehicle had the simple, clean lines of a Crosley, and had approximately the interior dimensions of a Volkswagen 'Beetle.' It had three wheels and detachable wings, with double rudders.

It was dubbed the Hall Flying Car, and after a successful test flight, was featured in a 1946 issue of *Popular Science* magazine. An offer for production was made by Portable Products Corporation in Garland, Texas, but this was not brought to fruition. Meanwhile, Consolidated Vultee, renamed Convair in 1946, was suffering a post-war sag in production, and was looking for a means to boost its profits.

conventional, car-like four-wheel configuration and a single rudder. The company designated it as the Convair Model 118 ConvAirCar. In July of 1946, Ted Hall and a Convair test pilot test flew the ConVairCar at 2000 feet (610 meters), made a couple of circles over the airfield and landed it successfully.

Convair management predicted minimum sales of 160,000 units with a retail price tag of US $1500, plus an extra charge for the wings—which would also be available for rental at any airport. However, another version, with further improvements, was to be built first.

This ConVairCar incorporated a fiberglass body that was to be standard on production models. It also had a 190-hp Pratt & Whitney radial engine with which it could attain speeds of up to 125 mph (201 kph) in the air. In 1947, disaster struck. This second ConVairCar took off on a routine flight, and the pilot misjudged his fuel. Forced to make an emergency landing on a dirt road, the ConVairCar sheared its wings off on overhanging trees.

The fiberglass body was beyond repair. Adverse publicity soon flooded the news media. This—combined with the postwar market glut of surplus light planes—prompted Convair to abandon the project. They sold the hardware back to Ted Hall, who is said to have retired to New York, though the two ConVAirCars are generally believed to be in a warehouse in El Cajon, California.

This really spelled the end of marketability for the flying car. If Convair, with its many resources, couldn't make a viable flying car, then nobody could. It's just as well. Imagine the sky clouded with thousands of flying machines piloted by people who would be as careless in the air as they are on the highway: the roofing industry would enjoy a long-term boom in business, but accident insurance costs would also soar.

Above: *An advertisement for the original Hall Flying Car (also, see the caption on Page 58)—which had a three-wheel, twin-tailboom configuration.*

Below: *An illustration of the original Hall Flying Car in 'roadable' configuration. The shaft on the nose of the car is the propeller shaft, linked to the main drivetrain of the car.*

One engine ran both propeller and wheels, and both were powered during take-off, for an extra 'boost.'

All market indicators seemed to point toward the success of the personalized airplane, and every major airplane maker in the US hoped to cash in on it. Therefore, when Hall approached his former employer with his flying car design, Consolidated Vultee/Convair bought him out, and prepared their main plant at San Diego's Lindbergh Field for development of the Hall Flying Car.

The company was so convinced that they had a potential success on their hands that they bought the Stinson Aircraft Company as a conduit for producing and marketing the Hall Flying Car, and also bought the Stout Aircraft Company, the manufacturer of the Skycar.

Convair developed an updated version of the Hall Flying Car. This version had a

THEY MIGHT HAVE BEEN GREAT

This is a chapter devoted to those automakers who had great ideas that failed to achieve proper fruition. This type of dilemma has traditionally arisen in one of several ways— either by running out of funds before design perfection can be achieved; or by getting sidetracked by an abiding, parallel interest, to the detriment of design functionality; or by simply having an idea at the wrong time.

pointment when, at the end of World War I, the German aircraft industry was virtually outlawed by the Treaty of Versailles.

He once again turned to the designing of cars. Even so, he was almost totally consumed with a private vision of a massive 10-engine transoceanic airplane. This, he would never realize—but it kept the spark of flight alive in him. Indeed, this spark was so strong that Rumpler infused his automotive designs with such aircraft-like aspects that they would have

1919–25 Rumpler Tropfen-Auto

The Tropfen-Autos featured streamlining that, though strange even today, was *effectively* far in advance of their contemporaries, and had ground-breaking mechanical features that, had they been further worked out, might have propelled the Tropfen-Autos beyond the mere shades of interest that they provoked in auto designers and engineers of their day.

The Tropfen-Autos were, in a sense, defeated by their many departures from what was then the norm, and in another sense, were too hybridized to overcome the sense that they were machines lost from their true element. More than any other auto in this text—save the flying cars—the Tropfen-Autos embodied the influence that aircraft development has had on the automobile.

Be that as it may, the Tropfen-Auto was a combination of some very good—and some very incongruous—ideas. The designer of these unusual cars was Edmund Rumpler, a mechanical engineer who was a pioneer in the German aircraft industry. Indeed, Rumpler's inspiration to become an engineer was a vision of heavier-than-air flight before such existed.

He was chief engineer for several turn-of-the-century automakers, including the Austro-Hungarian firm that would later become Tatra, where he met and encouraged the young Hans Ledwinka (see the text on Tatra cars). Rumpler also invented the swing axle and the transaxle. Even so, his automotive efforts were mere placebo for his burning desire to design airplanes.

When, at last, the time was ripe, with the Wright Brothers' aeronautical achievements, Rumpler plunged into the manufacture and design of aircraft, achieving renown with his upgrading of the Taube design. Great was his disap-

Opposite: A full-size Rumpler Tropfen-Auto, with hinged windshields and a single, cyclopean headlight. While its identifying placard proclaims it as a 1921 model, it is actually a 1925 Model 10/50.

This observation is bolstered by the fact that its fenders have departed from the minimal Rumplerian norm, and are actually miniatures of conventional period fenders. This was a feature of late Rumpler cars, especially 10/50s of 1924, when such 'compromise' indicated that the end was near.

That the steering wheel is not centrally located also confirms that this is a later Rumpler car, as does the single, dominant headlight: Tropfen-Autos of 1921 generally had two headlights, one larger, one smaller, arranged vertically.

been more successful had he mounted wings and propellers on them.

In early 1919, he embarked on the design of the Rumpler Tropfen-Auto. 'Tropfen' literally means 'to drip,' and suggested a drop sliding effortlessly through the air. Rumpler's patent on the Tropfen-Auto was applied for on 17 July 1919, and was granted on 30 December 1921. In overview, this first Tropfen-Auto was in essence the fuselage of an airplane.

The stamped-sheetmetal chassis was

also aircraft-like, closely following the contours of the body. This chassis was closed at its top by the floor of the body, and at the bottom by an underpan. Two spare tire/wheel assemblies were stowed in the intermediate space.

This car's profile was much like the flying boats of the day, with flattened central surfaces and an odd, upturned snout. Instead of dorsal wings or a windscreen, however, there was a cowl-like bump. The driver sat centrally forward, like a pilot, and behind the driver/pilot's

seat was a pair of single seats. Behind these was a bench seat.

Abutting the bench seat was the fire-wall, and beyond this was the rear-mounted engine-transaxle power train. However, with the engine, firewall and rear seat all in close contact, the rear seat passengers were sure to be roasted by the engine heat. The engine housing sloped down to the rear, and was perfo-rated with air-induction and heat-exhaust louvers.

Passengers in this open car faced the full frontal blast of wind. A variant on this design was effected by an addendum to Rumpler's patent, featuring a car that had vestigial, winglike fenders and a crude windscreen that encompassed the cockpit.

When a prototype was built, it was of the first patent design, with winglike fenders added, and no windscreen. It had two headlights, one above the other. The leading edges of the front fenders were fitted with running lights, and the cowl-like front of the car sported a winged Icarus—the symbol of Rumpler Werke AG, and a Rumplerian summation of the old human desire to transcend the Earth by human invention: ie, an airplane.

Rumpler's next patent was a further addendum, and specified a streamlined, enclosed passenger compartment, the roof of which curved like the dorsal sur-face of an airplane wing. This roof also sloped down to the sides, in an effort to eliminate turbulence. The car bearing this innovation was designated rather aeronautically as Model OA-104 proper. It was introduced to the public with the open car (Model 10/30 OA-104), at the Berlin Air Show of 1921.

Their revolutionary shapes caused a sensation—not all of it positive. One impression suggested by the hardtop was that of an enclosed dirigible gon-dola. The unusual Tropfen-Auto drive train proved to be of most interest: Benz & Cie bought options on the Tropfen-Auto design, and produced four tor-pedo-shaped racing prototypes that emulated the Tropfen-Auto transaxle and rear-engine placement.

Ferdinand Porsche was later to improve upon this drive train design with his Auto-Union racing cars of 1934, and other of his projects.

As for the efficiency of the enclosed car's streamlining, Rumpler and his chief aircraft dynamicist, Ludwig Prantdl, tested scale models of a Tropfen-Auto and a conventional car, and found the former to have a drag reduction of 60 percent over the latter.

The Models 10/30 OA-104 and OA-104 proper were smaller than the original, and clearly were intended as down-scale models for the marketplace. Model 10/30 OA-104, the open car, and Model OA-104, the closed car, had short, 114-inch (2.9-meter) wheelbases, with a driver's seat slightly offset to the right, and a tiny jump seat on the left of this. The jump seat would have been impossible to sit in, considering that all floor space in front of the driver was taken up with the four operating pedals. For normal pas-senger use, there was a single bench seat to the rear.

In profile, these shorter Tropfen-Autos also resembled flying boats, with a verti-cal, slightly curved nose and a gracefully curving rear. These cars were much like

Below: Isometric views of closed and open short-wheelbase Tropfen-Autos.

These cars shared a 114-inch (2.9-meter) wheelbase and early models were powered by a 141-ci (2.3-liter) version of Rumpler's overcomplicated and unsuccessful W-6 powerplant.

Fuel storage was in the nose of these smaller cars—not so good for a landgoing vehicle. The 'wing-roof' profile is clearly dis-cernible here.

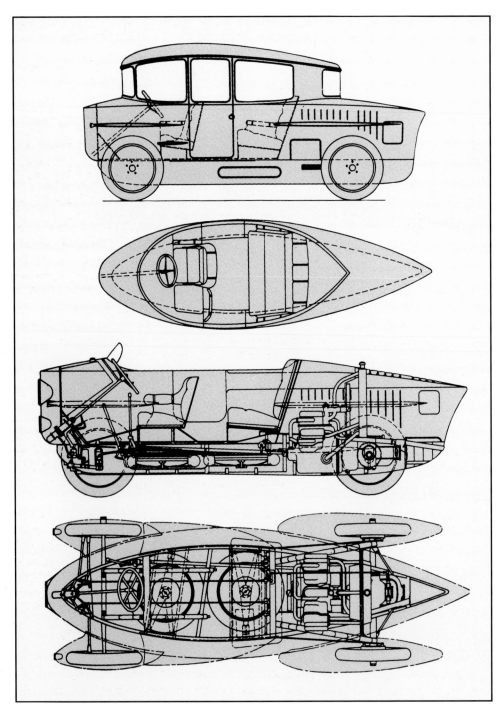

the previous Tropfen-Autos, with a small degree of heat relief having been brought to the rear seat by moving the firewall a few inches from the engine. The open car had a number of designations, *tourenwagen, offenerwagen* and *reise-wagen*—or 'touring car,' 'open car' and 'riding car'—while the closed car was called a limousine.

Unfortunately, Rumpler's small Trop-fen-Autos had their fuel storage in their noses, just behind the headlights. Additionally, none of the open cars had roofs, convertible or otherwise, and sported the tiniest of windshields—which might have kept dust from getting in the driver's mouth, but little else.

The powerplant that drove the early Tropfen-Autos was designed by Rumpler himself. It was an unusual, and unsuccessful, W-6 engine, with three banks of two cylinders each, of 141 cubic inches (2.3 liters) for the smaller cars; and 150 cubic inches (2.5 liters) for the larger cars; with 36 hp in either size. Cooling was enhanced in Models 10/30 OA-104 and OA-104 proper, and later cars, by a radiator and a long-bladed fan.

Rumpler launched into building larger Tropfen-Autos as a full-scale venture in 1922, fitting both open and closed bodies to the longer-wheelbase chassis. These cars were designated (confusingly enough) simply as Model 10/30. They seated five, but had only two doors—a clumsy solution to ingress and egress that imitated the hatch arrangements in large aircraft of the period.

In 1924, Rumpler abandoned the troublesome W-6 engine, and replaced it with a 158-cubic-inch (2.6-liter) in-line four, which produced 50 hp. Though the engine bore Rumpler's name on its rocker cover, its was probably a Benz, as it lacked Rumpler's highly inefficient trademark touch, in which both valves on each cylinder were closed by a single leaf spring.

This economy of design at the expense of actual function was—as we have seen with windshields, seating placement and doorway arrangements—one of the chief problems with the Tropfen-Autos. Also, the front cantilever springs were somewhat splayed in early Tropfen Autos, but in later models, these springs were brought inboard, and were completely out of the airstream. This contributed to pronounced body roll—not a recommended characteristic for a car whose slippery contours encouraged speed.

The cars' handling characteristics in general—already exacerbated by the design's very high center of gravity—

were not helped by the fact that the driver sat with his front feet beyond the front axle, as in truck-vans of the period, and the more recent Volkswagen 'Microbus.'

The Tropfen-Autos equipped with the four-cylinder engine were known as Model 10/50. On these, the steering wheel was at last moved over to the left, allowing a rational amount of room for a passenger up front beside the driver, and four doors were built into the body, providing adequate access for all passengers.

Among the Model 10/50s was an open car that had a full windshield—an aircraft-like wraparound windshield, without divider bars. This car also sported a strictly ornamental folded convertible roof. No Rumpler open car had a true convertible roof, as indeed, no airplane did: perhaps such a roof would have been too much concession to land travel.

In the Rumpler transaxle, both axles were live, and considerable transverse scrubbing of the rear tires was produced in cornering. Yet, this design served as inspiration for such as the legendary Porsche cars and the many rear-engine competition cars that have made racing history, not to mention the Volkswagen; and numerous front-wheel-drive designs using derivative transaxles.

The transaxle was a design whose very compactness mimicked the space-saving engine-to-propeller arrangements to be found in airplanes, thus holding a special attraction for this man who was, after all, an aeronautical engineer first and foremost.

Tropfen-Auto brakes were on par with the often eccentric setups of the early 1920s. Though arrangements differed from model to model, in general, Tropfen-Autos were equipped with front-wheel brakes, hand-operated emergency brakes on the rear wheels and a foot-operated 'driveshaft' brake. The 'driveshaft' in this case was a stub that extended beyond the final-drive housing. Curiously, later Tropfen-Autos eliminated the front wheel brakes.

Beyond the models we have mentioned, there were at least a dozen variants of the larger Tropfen-Autos. Indeed one was found to have an ultra-long wheelbase of 140 inches (3.6 meters), and was fitted with an American Continental L-head engine.

On some variants, the greenhouse-like top extended only about two-thirds of the way back toward the tail; on others, the greenhouse enclosed the tail. Some had clear glass all the way around; and

Above: *Truth in advertising? This advertisement of 1922 seems to say that a gentleman's hat would not fly off, and all passengers would remain not only unruffled, but dust-free, despite the almost total absence of a windshield in the open Tropfen-Auto design.*

Note the 'front and center' position of the driver's seat, and the flipperlike fenders—like nascent wings. Viewed from above like this, the Rumpler car's lozenge shape is most apparent.

With larger wings and a propeller, it would have flown. The winged figure at the top left of the ad is said to have represented Icarus—one might have wished Daedalus instead.

others, a luggage storage space with 'cupboard doors' instead of glass behind the passenger compartment. Some had opaque glass in the aft window frames, allowing no rear vision.

There were usually one or two headlights—always in the over-and-under, cyclopean arrangement. Doors were another matter. One long-wheelbase limousine with a partition between passenger and chauffeur compartments had a chauffeur's door that was barely large enough for a child, and required clambering over the fender to enter it, just as fighter plane pilots of the day had to climb over the wings of their aircraft to enter the cockpit.

Seating arrangements included the Rumplerian standard three single seats and bench seat; and another setup had one single seat (for the driver) and a wraparound bench seat that would have been barely able to accommodate three people due to lack of leg room.

Step-plates alternated with full running boards between variants, and some had stubby, winglike fenders, while some had semi-curved clamshell fenders. The last variants had very narrow conventional-style fenders—which seemed a grudging compromise of the essentially aeronauti-

cal design, and might have been more of a concession to the motorcar than Rumpler could countenance: he dropped the Tropfen-Auto idea shortly afterward, in 1925, and sold his shops in 1926.

However, in later years, he did design several front-wheel-drive vehicles based on the transaxle—one of which was a streamlined truck that made it clear that Rumpler had never given up on aircraft. The truck looked much like the fuselage of an airplane, with a conventional truck hood and grille added on the front like an afterthought. Cosmetic creases on either side of the forward surfaces depicted the nose of an airplane quite clearly.

Rumpler worked for Chrysler overseas operations for a while, and then, in the turmoil of the Third Reich, was put to work on a 'people's car' project that was probably the Volkswagen. Edmund Rumpler died at home in 1940, at the age of 68.

Rumpler's experiments left a legacy of streamlining for others to follow—which they dutifully did, producing such automobiles as the Tatra and the Chrysler Airflow, to name two streamliners that also appear in this text (please see). Of course, Rumpler hadn't been the first to

Below: A Rumpler Tropfen-Auto of the original, open design that had no windshield. This design suggests an early flying boat, and only the wheels are a sure tipoff that this is a vehicle meant for the road.

The 'wing-roof' design came almost as an afterthought, but after windtunnel tests, Rumpler discerned that the closed cars had a 60 percent lower drag resistance than the open cars.

Thus, the closed cars were considered by the Rumplerian inner circle to be the only 'true' Tropfen-Autos.

build streamliners, he simply had made a few unique contributions.

Decades passed, and by the end of World War II, the world found itself in the Jet Age. Some automakers, suffused with the excitement of the new field of jet aircraft engineering, turned their attentions to new modes of power for automobiles.

1950 Rover Whizzard

The Rover Whizzard was a turbine-engine car, and was first unveiled at Silverstone Airport, in England, in 1950. That such a conservative automaker as Rover would come out with a turbine car was a sign of the times, and in a sense, the car was a product of the transportation industry as a whole.

The question of motive power—not only for cars, but for airplanes and railroad trains—was much debated at the time. With aircraft, the advent of the turbine-jet engine promised a bright future,

as jet aircraft attained previously unattainable speeds. Railroads were experimenting with steam turbines—in an attempt to salvage a century's worth of investment in steam power, which was being pushed into obsolescence by diesel-electric technology.

The automotive industry was facing a need for ever more efficient powerplants that would deliver good performance even in lower-priced cars—thanks to the improvements in highways, and a post-war milieu that emphasized power and speed. While many automakers thought in terms of the piston engine, some automakers contemplated joining the turbine bandwagon.

If steam pistons could be replaced with turbine blades in a locomotive, why not in an automobile engine? It would be wonderful for sales, too—directly borrowing the then-tremendous glamor of the jet aircraft as well.

Thus the impetus was supplied for Rover to design and realize a turbine engine for their Whizzard. This somewhat bulbous, open-canopy car represented a few modifications on the basic Rover shape of the time. The turbine-

Above: *The Rover Whizzard Gas Turbine car. Among other things, it was a 'wizard' at making fuel disappear from its gas tank. Also known as 'Jet 1,' the Whizzard could accelerate to 93 mph (150 kph), but got a miserable five miles (eight km) to the gallon of gasoline.*

While undoubtedly powerful, turbines were unduly thirsty, and subsequent Rover Turbine cars–the Jet 2 sedan and the T4, failed to solve the problem.

Above: *The Chrysler Turbine Car of 1963. Styled and engineered by Chrysler Corporation, it was hand-crafted by Ghia of Italy.*

The publicity for this car proclaimed, rather cryptically, that the turbine engine 'delivered 130 hp, but rendered overall performance equal to a V-8 engine of more than 200 hp.' Perhaps this was a way of saying that the turbine engine swallowed tankfuls of fuel like a big V-8.

engined Whizzard, aka 'Jet 1,' could achieve 93 mph (150 kph), but it was gas-hungry, getting only five miles (eight km) to the gallon of fuel.

This great thirst was a distinct disadvantage, coupled with the probable costs of retooling to mass-produce turbine engines that did not as yet enjoy clearly marketable advantages over piston engines.

However, Rover was awarded the DeWar Trophy for their engineering daring in making the attempt, and the company therefore went ahead with another turbine project, the 'Jet 2,' which featured a somewhat upgraded turbine in a cute little sedan body, and was the focal point of much company publicity.

Then, in 1961, Rover brought out the very modern-looking T4, which seemed to have borrowed much of its styling from the large-body Citroen school. The Rover

Company claimed that it had almost solved the turbine problem with this car, and, as if to prove their point, ran a turbine car at Le Mans—and then ran another at Le Mans!

However, the Rover turbine car for the masses was not to be, as the T4 was the last domestic turbine car that Rover attempted. Costs of development were simply too much, and the car's performance did not justify its heavy fuel consumption.

The 1950s and the 1960s were, in their way, as daring and inventive as any other period in automotive history had been. Included in this yen for innovation were still other intensive studies of alternative powerplants.

In fact, Chrysler, Ford and General Motors each had a prototype turbine car in the 1950s. Then, at the turn of the decade and with the space race in full

swing, Chrysler Corporation's sales needed a boost. Perhaps that is why the corporation sought to tie its name to the excitement of advanced 'space age' technology—even if that technology had been attempted before.

1963 Chrysler Turbine Car

Chrysler's first turbine car experiment had involved the placement of a 100-hp turbine engine in an otherwise stock 1956 Plymouth Belvedere. This established that such a feat could be done, but some years would lapse before a more serious venture was tried.

The Chrysler Turbine of 1963 was the result of extensive experimentation with using turbine (as opposed to piston) power to turn an automotive driveshaft. This car was designed by Elwood Engle, who had just previously styled the Ford Thunderbirds of the early 1960s. Chrysler had the bodies for this sleek, limited-production automobile built by Ghia, of Italy.

With a wheelbase of 110 inches (2.8 meters), and a curb weight of 3900 pounds (1773 kg), the Chrysler Turbine Car was comparable to other upscale two-door sedans of the early 1960s.

Fifty of these cars were built. Each was assigned a three-month trial period with voluntary temporary owners. The cars had respectable performance, going from 0 to 60 mph (0 to 96 kph) in 10 seconds. Gas economy was very bad, however, and 12 mpg (19 kpg) seemed to be the best the turbine engine could achieve. (Also, turbines tend to run hot, with interior temperatures of 1375 degrees Fahrenheit [782 degrees Celsius], giving off exhaust gases of 525 degrees Fahrenheit [274 degrees Celsius].)

The Chrysler turbine engine had 80 percent fewer moving parts than a piston engine, and generated 130 horsepower. Chrysler rather cryptically claimed that their turbine delivered performance equal to a 200-hp piston engine. As we have seen, however, it consumed gasoline like a *300*-hp piston engine.

The very idea of the car, with its jet-age associations and tastefully futuristic styling, could have worked either for or against it in terms of sales. Chrysler had to consider what the gas-hogging, groundbreaking car would do for them that the Airflow—an infamous groundbreaker—hadn't done.

With a beautiful body, the Turbine Car would probably not suffer the Airflow's fate exactly. But, with the costs of retooling, and with the echoes of Ford's then-recent attempt to bring out an all-new model—the Edsel—still ringing in tones

of calumny, Chrysler was not about to take the plunge.

Chrysler Corporation terminated the project, destroying 40 of the expensively-built Turbine Cars to avoid import duty on their Italian-built bodies. The remaining 10 cars went to museums throughout the US. With the gasoline crisis of the 1970s not far in the future—and with it, the federal Corporate Average Fuel Economy restrictions—the ultimate failure of the Turbine Car project was perhaps predestined.

Other alternative powerplants also caught manufacturers' imaginations. It was seen that one of the main factors in conventional piston engine failures was the large number of moving parts in same.

An answer seemed to come via the designs of a European engineering genius. Here was a promise of simplicity and efficiency that would revolutionize motoring at least as much as had the wholsesale embracing of the overhead-valve engine in the 1950s.

Below: A rear view of the Chrysler Turbine Car. The roof was covered with black vinyl—which was considered to be très chic *in the 1960s—and the rear-end styling was meant to evoke whirling turbines and a swept-back, Jet Age look.*

After extensive testing, 40 of the original run of 50 cars were destroyed to avoid import tax, with the survivors going to museums.

1964 NSU Wankel Spider

This was the first Wankel-engined car. The Wankel engine is a rotary powerplant that uses an internal shaft with lobes that form combustion chambers, and hence combines the principles of the turbine and the piston.

This hybrid was invented by Dr Felix Wankel for whom it is named. He intended it to be an answer to the perceived inefficiencies of the piston engine. Dr Wankel felt that direct rotary action as a driving force for cars was one step up from imparted rotary action (as is the case with the conventional 'pistons-pumping-driveshaft-turning' setup). The eccentric rotor spins inside an eccentric combustion chamber, and imparts its torque to an eccentric driveshaft.

The first Wankel engines were single-rotor designs, and had an unbalanced feel when tested. The as-yet crude engine suffered from myriad problems, including failure of the chamber seal at the tip of the rotor.

However, NSU of West Germany became interested in the engine, and worked with Dr Wankel to develop a car for the engine. The result was the NSU Wankel Spider of 1964. It was a handsome little two-seater with a top speed of around 90 mph (145 kph).

However, it was hugely unreliable: most of all, the Wankel engine failed due to oil leakage and rotor-tip seal failure. The engines 'blew up,' as the jargon goes, after 10,000 miles (10,900 km), and NSU's expenditure for new machinery to produce the engines was wasted.

But NSU was not so easily defeated. They went ahead with another Wankel program.

Above: *An NSU Wankel Spider. With a tiny rotary powerplant of 61-ci (one-liter) capacity, it used gasoline at a rate of 20 miles (32 km) per gallon—a thirst equal to engines three times its size.*

Worse yet, the engine would self-destruct after approximately 10,000 miles (10,900 km) of use. This single-rotor version of Dr Felix Wankel's design suffered imbalance problems and rotor-tip seal failure.

Above opposite: *A rear-mounted Wankel engine in an NSU Spider sports car.*

Above: *An NSU Ro80 four-door sedan. The base power plant for the Ro80 was a twin-rotor Wankel engine. It was very powerful but very unreliable: the company had to replace entire engines for its customers after 10–20,000 miles (10,900– 21,800 km) of use.*

Opposite: *The Mercedes-Benz C-111 sports coupe. The C-111 had a triple-rotor Wankel engine mounted just behind the seats. It was sleek and fast, but had too many complications to justify a production model.*

1967 NSU Ro80

This was NSU's last rotary-engine automobile. For this venture, NSU developed a 105-hp twin-rotor Wankel engine. This engine was potent beyond its ratings, and seemed to have unlimited rpms. It was, however, totally unreliable.

At first, optimism ran high. Fitted into the advanced-looking Ro80 body and chassis, the Wankel appeared to have found a home. The Ro80 looked more like a car of the present day than of the 1960s. The engine, however, tended to suffer failure of such magnitude that it had to be *replaced* every 10–20,000 miles (10,900–32,180 km), and such replacement was extravagantly expensive.

NSU was still paying for the retooling it had undertaken to·produce the Wankel engine en masse. Therefore, as terrible as the car was for buyers, it was even more

so for the company that produced it. NSU eventually had to merge with Volkswagen to keep its leaking economic ship afloat. 'No more Wankels' was an unspoken, but understood, condition of the merger. Even so, another West German Wankel project was taking shape.

1969 Mercedes-Benz C-111

The Wankel engine, with its promise of simplicity and great acceleration, enchanted automakers around the world despite its failures. The next automakers to give the Wankel engine a try were Rolls-Royce and Mercedes-Benz—the latter of which produced a sports coupe, the C-111, which was very sleek and very fast.

Premature breakdowns ended the C-111's promise. Rolls-Royce tested and re-tested their Wankel concept, only to back away from the engine's problems. Then, General Motors made a bold pronouncement that they would have a Wankel-engined car for the market by 1974, but this did not come to be.

Then, in much the same way that NSU offered its research treasury upon the altar of innovation, at least one Japanese manufacturer also suffered.

1970–75 Mazda

Having developed a three-rotor (and better-balanced) version of the revolutionary Wankel rotary engine, Mazda used it as a selling point for their product. At first it seemed that Mazda had made a smart move, as the new engine had a high horsepower-to-engine-displacement ratio. True, it was not an economy engine, with gas mileage similar to high-performance conventional powerplants of larger displacement, but the power produced by the Wankel seemed to more than compensate for that shortcoming.

However, as with the case of the NSU Spider, the Mazda rotary engine had not been perfected. The tiny seals at the tips of the Wankel rotor were very difficult items to make reliable, and one after another, they failed.

Above and above opposite: *Mazda RX-3 series models, including station wagons, sedans and sport coupes. The same cars, when equipped with a five-speed transmission, were designated 'RX-4.'*

Breakdowns were frequent, and gas mileage was very bad. Ironically, Mazda advertising hyped them as having 'the same, proven, high-performance rotary engine as the RX-2s....'

Below opposite: *A Mazda RX-2 sport coupe. It was the first full-production Mazda rotary, with lots of power—when it ran.*

Below: *The limited-production Mazda R130 coupe, one of the first Mazda rotary-engined cars, looked a lot like an Audi. The early Mazda rotaries matched the NSU cars for mechanical instability.*

It was a frustrating situation, for even as a Wankel-equipped Mazda passed car after car on the interstate one day, the very next, it would be laid up in the shop, and its owner was forced to ride the bus.

The problems with Mazda rotaries of this period were legendary, and to add yet more weight to the millstone of despair, environmental emissions controls in the large US market were getting stricter, presenting an increasingly difficult barrier for the rather 'dirty' Wankel. Even worse, transmissions and clutches were also disastrously prone to failure on 1970–75 Mazda rotary-equipped cars.

Mazda continued their rotary lines even after the debacles up to and including 1975, but did not offer them in some export markets. After much brainstorming, Mazda came out with a much more reliable, economical and emissions-efficient engine, and introduced the Wankel-engined RX-7 sports coupe in 1980, and it was a success. In 1986, a new generation of RX-7s took over from that line, and has also been successful.

For the record, 1970–75 Mazda rotaries were built, variously, on 91-, 97- and 99-inch (2.3-, 2.4- and 2.5-meter) wheelbases—in four-door sedan, sport coupe and four-door wagon configurations, with major designations progressing from RX to RX-3, and additional five-speed offerings designated RX-4 that were concomitant with the RX-3s, and included a pickup truck variant on a 104-inch (2.6-meter) wheelbase.

FROM THE BIZARRE TO THE OVERDONE

1947–49 Davis

Davis Motor Car Company of Van Nuys, California, produced the infamous Davis automobiles. The first Davises were four-passenger, two-door coupes with removable hardtops. They were powered by 46-horsepower, 132-cubic-inch (2.2 liters) Hercules four-cylinder engines, and were 185 inches (4.7 meters) in overall length.

Later Davises were powered by a four-cylinder Continental 'flathead' engine of 162 cubic inches (2.6 liters) and 57 horsepower. There was also a military prototype produced. The entire production life of the Davis Motor Car Company stretched from 1947 to 1949.

The Davis was a three-wheel car with such radical styling that the front bumper was a razor-edged 'Vee,' and its profile, with a low-mounted, mouthlike grille vent, made one think of a sleeping killer whale. This car was highly publicized, as it seemed an exciting advance for automotive technology—at the time.

One of its selling points was the promised capability of executing a sudden, full-lock turn at 55 mph (88 kph). This was demonstrated by Company President GG 'Gary' Davis. However, the speed was exaggerated, as, when the car was put through such turns, the drive wheel would lift, lose traction and spin in freely,

so the speedometer could thus be made to indicate a higher speed than the car had actually achieved.

This car's engineering was such that it was top-heavy, and too much weight rested on the lone front wheel. Despite promises of 116 mph (186 kph) top end and 30 mpg (48 kpg) economy, the actual maximums were 65 mph (105 kph) and 28 mpg (45 kpg).

The Davis company became embroiled in a financing scandal, and closed its doors in 1949. However, Davis was certainly not the last automaker to seek new horizons in automotive design.

Below: *A 1949 Davis four-person coupe with removable hardtop in place. That sharp front bumper could give your shin a nasty crack.*

In fast turns, the Davis three-wheeler would heel over on two wheels, lifting the third. This propensity, which caused highly misleading speedometer readings, was exploited by Davis promotions—please see the text, these pages.

From the photograph opposite, it is easy to trace the major styling influence of the Davis car. Once you got past the 'tricycle' running gear, however, the similarity ended, despite the Davis Car Company's claims.

Powered by one of two L-head engines of 46 and 57 hp, the Davis car was definitely not a landlocked jet.

1949–54 Nash Airflyte

Nash had been a respected manufacturer of cars since the 1930s. While its products were not overwhelmingly innovative, such models as the 482-R of the 1930s were strikingly handsome machines. Unfortunately, Ford Motor Company and General Motors Corporation had so flooded the market with their cars that they had established their concepts as the norm, and it took an extravagant effort—such as the terrible but ultimately influential Chrysler Airflow—to shock the market into changing.

Nash had never been one to remain in the rear of the conceptual pack, either. In 1941, Nash followed the lead of Cord and Lincoln, and introduced a car with unit-body construction, coil springs all around and sliding-pillar independent front suspension, *a la* the Lancia of Italy.

With the advent of World War II and the subsequent diversion of automakers to the production of war materials, no cars were made and after the war, the larger automakers—Chrysler, Ford and

Above: *A 1950 Nash Airflyte Ambassador Custom sedan, representative of the worst automotive styling fiasco since the Chrysler Airflow cars of the 1930s.*

Note the beetling profile and the imprisoned-looking wheels. There was no such thing as making a tight turn with an Airflyte.

General Motors—essentially relied on revamped pre-war designs to tide sales over until newer designs could be wrought.

This gave smaller companies like Nash a chance to grab the lead—if only they could come up with sufficiently fresh designs. What Nash felt was such a design emerged from the Nash stables as the pet project of Nash President George F Mason and Chief Engineer Meade F Moore. This was the ultra-compact Metropolitan, strictly a town car that had room for two, a four-cylinder Austin 42 hp engine, and a diminutive 85-inch (2.1-meter) wheelbase.

Designed by independent stylist Bill Flajole, the tiny car was essentially a rounded box, with a choice of hardtop or convertible roof, and a two-tone (always white on top) color scheme. The bodies were built in England by the firm of Fisher and Ludlow.

All public reactions to its exhibition showings had been positive, and its unit-body construction was one of its selling points. In fact, it was to be a very success-ful little car. The Metropolitan could attain 70 mph (113 kph) and was extremely economical. Introduced for sale in 1953, as of 1959 the made-overseas Metropolitan was second only to Volks-wagen in imported car sales in the US, with 20,435 units sold.

Pre-sale car show reaction to the Met-ropolitan was so good that Nash took its next gamble, a daring plunge into streamlining. Thus, George Mason and company came out in 1949 with a style for their large cars—the Ambassador and the Statesman—called Airflyte.

Airflyte was as infamous a styling move as had been the Chrysler Airflow. True, the Airflyte cars were reasonably good mechanically, possessing a reliable and smooth, if a little subdued, six-cylinder engine. Nash also came up with a num-ber of features that made these cars very popular with travelling salesmen and sportsmen—the most prized of which was the option of folding the front seat backward to form a bed, in combination with the back seat.

Unfortunately, fender cutouts for the

wheel wells were nonexistent, and the front wheels were thus constricted in their movements. The Nash Airflyte could make no claims as to a tight turning radius.

The single feature that made Airflyte Nash cars anathema to many motorists was the beetling silhouette that emblemized what have been called 'perhaps the unloveliest production cars ever built.'

Though there were other 'inverted bathtubs' being offered to the public—notably, the Packard and the Hudson—none approached the level of calamity that Nash styling had achieved.

While this styling debacle is generally blamed on Nils Wahlberg, a Nash engineer, the real culprit may well have been Norman Bel Geddes, who is most known for the model cars he built for the General Motors Futurama at the 1939 New York World's Fair. Geddes' vision of future transport tended toward bulbous designs with unlikely configurations—cars that seemed a cross between free-form bubbles and utility trucks.

Norman Bel Geddes is believed to have done his last design work under contract for Nash, where he produced a number of prototype models that probably influenced Wahlberg's concept of Airflyte styling, given that the Airflyte's emphasis on small, semi-hidden wheels, bubble-like 'fastback' and general homeliness evidenced heavy Geddesian influence.

The Airflyte styling was also applied to Nash's Rambler line, which bore the burden of Nash's bid for the nascent American economy market. The first year of the Airflyte Ramblers presented the Rambler Station Wagon and the Rambler All-Weather Convertible—a convertible whose 'safety feature' was that it had permanently upright door- and windowframes. Then came the Rambler Country Club, a landau coupe; the Greenbriar All-Purpose Sedan, a station wagon with emplaceable seats; and the Greenbriar Sedan, a standard four-door.

The Rambler Airflyte was introduced to the public in 1950. Smaller than the Nash Commodore and Statesman, the Rambler Airflyte styling was a little better suited to the smaller car.

The motivation behind Nash's choice of the Geddesian design probably lies in the Nash/Rambler advertising slogan: 'Before you decide, take an Airflyte ride—in the world's most modern car.' Nash was out to prove a point, but chose the wrong stylistic argument.

Even on the Rambler line, Airflyte styl-ing seemed self-contradictory, positing a new idea only to apologize for it by design quirks that were so bad they were sheer genius. It was as if R Buckminster Fuller's Dymaxion had mated with Rust Heinz's Phantom Corsair and produced offspring incorporating the dowdiest aspects of those two cars' oddball futurism.

From an affective point of view, even the most conservative of other automakers' designs—the basic Ford sedan, for example—produced an impression of optimism. The dominant sense conveyed by the Airflyte design was of something slightly curdled, or overcooked, stuffy and claustrophobic. Perhaps this was because each curve that might have aesthetically succeeded was blunted, bringing a sense of confinement to the styling of the car, as opposed to what might have been (in more capable hands) a dramatic tension-producing sense of aesthetic restraint.

Below: A frontal view of a 1950 Nash Ambassador Custom sedan. Like a grimacing chipmunk, the Airflyte 'look' greeted the observer with 'full cheek' fenders and an aesthetically painful, teeth-gnashing grille.

Overleaf: A 1949 Nash Airflyte 600 four-door sedan. The glistening white paint makes the design look extra-bulbous, and a second look reveals the eccentricities that made Airflytes a negative part of the American cultural subconscious.

If the hulking, chrome-lipped Buicks of the early 1950s could be said to 'bare their teeth' at onlookers, and Fords of the same era seemed to have a parsimonious moue ever implanted upon their grille-work, then the Nash looked as if it had seen (or undergone) something absolutely hideous, and its lips were parted in a grimace of existential pain.

Nash dropped the Airflyte styling in 1953, settling for a more conventional

notchback body style. The front wheels still stubbornly refused to come into the open, however, and hid behind the fenders sans wheelwell cutouts.

The company took over the failing Hudson firm in the mid-1950s, and produced a number of Hudson models that were identical to the Nashs, which had progressed to the conservative, slab-sided models of the late 1950s. These occasionally burst into flamboyance via large-hubbed wire wheels and glitzy attachments that seemed out of place, and both Nash and Hudson produced the tiny Metropolitan as a sidelight to their larger models.

Nash and Hudson went out of business in 1957, leaving the now-parent American Motors company with Rambler, which took great advantage of the burgeoning American recession, becoming the nation's small-car sales leader in the late 1950s–early 1960s.

Rambler produced designs that ran the gamut from the boxy cars of the late

1950s to the attractive lines of the American of the 1960s. Even in its post-Airflyte days, however, American Motors Corporation occasionally erupted in *outre* styling. Such, for example, was the Marlin of 1965, with its vast, radical fastback and otherwise conservative looks; and the Matador coupe of 1974–75, which resembled the blighted offspring of a manta ray and a bullfrog.

In fact, the Matador coupe was almost inexplicable. It was a frightening-looking automobile with goggling headlights and vast, radically sweeping body planes that proclaimed that the automaker was banking on 'futurism' once again, and had somehow stolen the frontal appearance of Lockheed's SR-71 Blackbird spy plane—great for a Mach 3 jet, but an awful thing to see looming out of the fog on a rainy workday morning!

This author feels that such odd design was due to periodic regressions to the Airflyte frame of mind—in which 'technology' obliterated aesthetics, as was

No vacancy? No problem—just sleep in a Nash! Below: *A promotional cutaway of an Airflyte sedan, with its most popular optional feature: the twin-bed conversion, available for just $39.*

Travelling salesmen and early-rising anglers loved the convenience. Even the occasional family was lured into purchasing a Nash Airflyte car.

However, this young father looks like he just can't forget the awful styling of the car in which he sleeps.

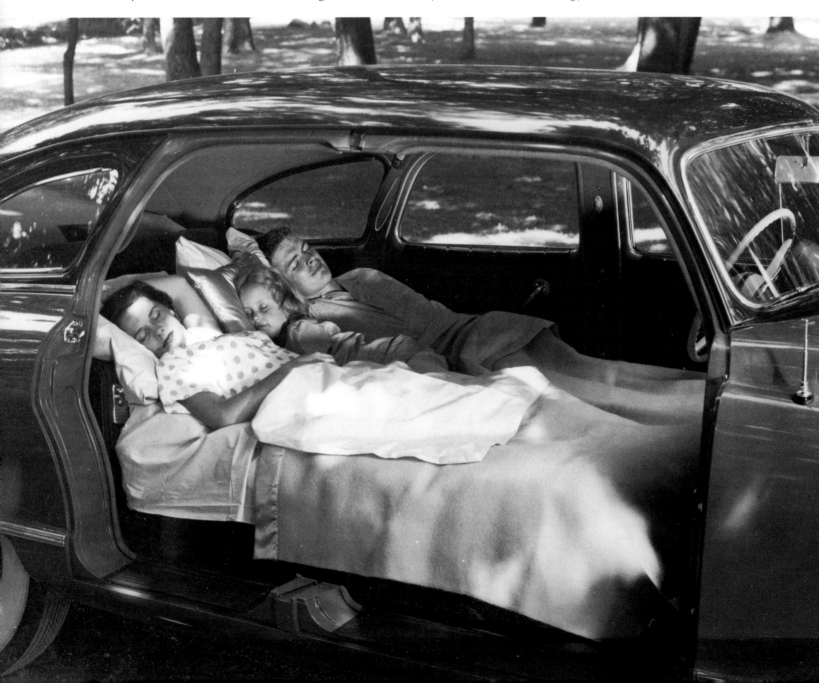

only to be expected in the Utopian atmosphere of the early post-war world.

In post-war Europe, economy was a very big selling point for automakers, as gasoline and carmaking materials were at a premium. This situation gave rise to a type of car that nearly went beyond economy, with barely sufficient powerplants to keep it moving, and barely enough carbody to shield its occupants.

These cars were popularly known as 'bubble cars,' because they most resembled bubbles, with no discernible sculpturing on the silhouette. Ironically, the later-beloved Volkswagen 'Beetle' was a top-of-the-line bubble car, just over the ragged edge of respectability.

1950s BMW Isetta

The prime example of the post-war bubble car was the BMW Isetta, a rear-engine two-seater with simple, sliding-panel side windows and a sunroof. On the sides of this gumdrop-shaped little car were amber safety lights, and forward of these were the vehicle's headlights, mounted on either side of the driver's compartment like the peripheral lights of a diving bell.

Extending from mid-way up the frontal fender surfaces of one variant were tubular bars that were bent down under the chassis, forming one of the most useless bumper arrangements ever devised: these left the front center of the car unprotected. This was but a minor flaw in the design of this wretched little car, for it had only one door, which also formed the nose of the car.

Yes, the front of the car was the only door the Isetta had. It opened out to the left, and the instrument panel was attached to it. The steering wheel was also attached to the door, and when egress was desired, the door was opened, and the steering column hinged outward to accommodate the action.

The interior handle was opposite the driver: in a front-end accident, the driver would likely be pinioned by the flimsy steering wheel, and would be unable to reach the door latch. Beyond that, any serious front end collision would very likely result in the deaths of driver and passenger, as there was no substantial structure to prevent the Isetta from crumpling front to rear like a piece of paper.

Should the occupants survive a head-on, there was no way short of smashing the windows to escape, as the only nor-mal egress was the (probably) jammed front door. Also, in those days before standardized seatbelts, there was nothing in the Isetta to keep the passenger (the driver being pinioned by the steering wheel) from hurtling through the front windshield.

Had the Isetta been a good-handling little machine, one could have driven (extremely) defensively, but its wide-front-narrow-back track widths were best suited to going in a straight line. Incidentally, those back wheels also steered the car, making this strange little car truly mechanically backward.

It was an oddly cute little car, but had about it more than the *air* of disaster.

Meanwhile, the economy car boom was starting to take hold in the US. Rambler was the best-selling American economy car, a fact that spurred the larger American automakers to develop such economy car designs as the Ford Falcon, the Chevrolet Corvair and the Dodge Lancer. The way was also open for imports to garner a share of the US market. Among these were the famous Volkswagen 'Beetle,' and several British offerings. The French were to have their say, too.

Above: *A 1956 BMW Isetta, showing the odd treadwidth design, as well as the one slim chance that passengers had of escaping this little deathtrap in the event of a collision—its single, front-mounted, door.*

Believe it or not, the bumper setup shown here was actually an improvement *over an alternate setup—for a description of which, see the text.*

These pages: *Views of a 1956 BMW Isetta, showing the door open, and closed, and a profile. Never much more than a motorcycle with a weather shell, it was steered by the narrow-set rear wheels, giving it the approximate maneuverability of a forklift-truck.*

The Isetta actually became odder as time went on, for in turn-of-the-decade models, the two rear wheels were replaced by one—making the Isetta a reverse tricycle, with steering relegated to the single rear wheel.

1956–68 Renault Dauphine

In the US, the ad jingle—which featured the unmistakable sound of this French car's horn—was 'Renault (beep!) (beep!) Dauphine!' Introduced to the US in 1959, the Renault Dauphine was similar in size and configuration to the Volkswagen 'Beetle,' but there the similarity ended.

Built to ride the crest of the postwar 'bubble car' craze, and first produced in 1956, the Renault Dauphine was the first French car to sell two million units in its time of production. It was equipped with a tiny 30-cubic-inch (485-cc) powerplant that was upgraded to 47 cubic inches (796 cc) in the late 1950s, and was again enlarged to 58 cubic inches (956 cc) in 1962.

The Dauphine's drawing card was obviously economy. However, its handling was quite unstable, as the car's high center of gravity and rear engine configuration made it a difficult vehicle to corner at speed or to control in crosswinds.

That the US was a prime market for small economy cars is evidenced by Renault's sales of 93,000 Dauphines there in 1959. However, the cute little cars were literally full of defects, with door handles that detached in the owners' hands, and a tendency toward undercarriage corrosion—especially in the sometimes harsh North American climate—that was so marked that American tow truck operators hesitated to tow Dauphines, as more than one, when hoisted by its front end, suffered undercarriage collapse.

The Dauphine thus managed to overcome its auspicious start and so blackened Renault's name in the US market that Renault abandoned most of its projects in the US in 1965. No matter that Renault had, in the interim, come up with superior models, and was to strike real gold with the advent of the Renault 16— an advanced, extremely versatile and reliable automobile—the Dauphine had done its damage.

The car was, however, continued into the late 1960s, during which time body metal was thickened, and the engine was changed once more to 51.5 cubic inches (845 cc) at 40 hp, with a 0 to 60 mph (0 to 97 kph) elapsed time of 34 to 36 seconds. That the Dauphine was the cheapest four-door economy car on the US market, and that it virtually sank out of sight in that market by the mid-1960s was telling enough.

Opposite: A 1959 Renault Dauphine sedan USA-export model. Built for the relatively mild climate of France, the Renault Dauphine met its Waterloo in North America.

Tipsy handling and undercarriage collapse due to corrosion were but two of the complaints that helped to drive the imported Dauphine out of the New World.

Previous pages: *A 1958 Edsel Pacer, the higher of the two lower-level Edsels (the other was the Edsel Ranger).*

In addition to these, there were upper-level, longer-wheelbase Edsels known as the Corsair and the Citation.

Ford Motor Company was so serious about its all-new Edsel that it established a complete division for the make before it even hit the market.

Untimely and eccentric design, plus a tendency toward too much gimmickry in the upper-range cars, spelled disaster for the Edsel Division.

Economy was one thing, but American citizens were also enthralled by the fantastic advances taking place in the realm of jet aircraft. Turbine car experiments notwithstanding (see the chapter 'They Might Have Been Great'), Americans were happily entering the Jet Age en masse: the Boeing Commercial Aircraft Company delivered the first commercial jet airliner, the Model 707, to Pan American Airlines in August of 1958.

In fact, Jet-Age styling had already made its mark on American cars. More than any other nation, the US threw itself into producing cars with jet-like fins, tons of chrome and taillights that imitated the fires of jet afterburners. From the 1949 Cadillac with its nascent tail fins, to the 1959 Chrysler New Yorker with its monstrous, sweeping dorsal appendages, the age of 'fins and chrome' was unforgettable—but there were limits to its appeal, as some automakers found out.

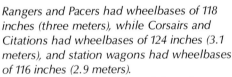

Rangers and Pacers had wheelbases of 118 inches (three meters), while Corsairs and Citations had wheelbases of 124 inches (3.1 meters), and station wagons had wheelbases of 116 inches (2.9 meters).

Above: A 1958 Edsel Corsair four-door hardtop, evidencing the special 'beauty inserts' that upper-levels Edsels wore in their side-body coves.

1958–60 Ford Edsel Ranger, Pacer, Corsair, Citation

General Motors was grabbing so big a share of the upper-middle-price auto market in the 1950s with their Pontiac, Oldsmobile and Buick ranges, Ford Motor Company decided to do something about it. The way to go, Ford decided, was to grab the public's attention with something really different. Given that this was an era of stylistic experimentation, 'something different' either meant a retreat to utter simplicity or an as-yet unthought-of direction in

which to take car design.

Ford, in what can only be described as design strategem of desperate genius, did both. Genius of course carries the caveat that it may present the radical departure, or the previously unseen subtlety, but it does not always harmonize with truth or success. Such was the case with this Ford product.

Mated to a body that was reasonably unpretentious was a yawning beak of a grille that made the casual observer think of a nestling bird gaping wide for a worm. In all fairness, this ovoid grille could also be said to resemble an eagle with its mouth open as it pursues its prey, or Basil Rathbone, as Sherlock Holmes, making a pronouncement between puffs on his pipe.

Set far to either side of this grille were quad headlights in pairs that bulged

upward and outward like the eyes of an infuriated corporate director, 'lording it' over the secondary, muted horizontal grillework that ran under them in subservient complement to the gaping maw at the center. The fenders were incongruously squared off: this squareness was emulated by the bright chrome bumper, which underscored the design's stunning failure to mate the curve and the angle.

A look at the rear of the car revealed taillights that were psychologically inspired, but odd-looking—horizontal strips of red glass that dipped down as they approached the central region of the vast trunk lid, and resembled the eyes of a man who is grimacing triumphantly at the car he's just passed. The trunk lid on convertible models called to mind the Great Plains of the US in its unbroken

expanse, and perhaps this was another psychological ploy to put distance between oneself and the traffic one had just left behind.

The project was begun at Henry Ford II's insistence, in 1952. It was felt that General Motors' overwhelming market share was due to its more numerous model lines. Ford had to catch up, and the only way was to build more models.

Hence, a project was begun whereby a whole new division of Ford Motor Company would be created to bring out the required models. Ford's Marketing Research Department then approached the renowned American poetess, Marianne Moore, thinking that she would surely come up with a name to match their grand design.

She did in fact come up with names that admirably suited this oddball

Above: *A three-quarter rear view of a 1958 Edsel Pacer, showing the rear lighting setup.*

The large taillights appeared to be grimacing triumphantly at all the cars the Edsel had just passed. With a 352-ci (5.8-liter) V-8 in lower-range Edsels, and 410-ci (6.7-liter) V-8s in upper-range Edsels, there was potential for a lot of 'grimacing.'

Overleaf: *A 1958 Edsel Citation convertible. The finish of this car is done in turquoise—a color much in vogue in the 1950s.*

A classic despite its being the center of the most expensive automotive failure of its time (Ford lost from $250–350 million), Edsels like this are prized possessions today.

Above: *A driver's-eye-view of an upper-level 1958 Edsel. Note the transmission selector buttons in the steering wheel hub, and the multitude of levers and switches on and around the dash panel.*

design, but her offerings were rejected. Among the names she proposed were 'The Utopian Turtletop,' 'The Resilient Bullet,' and 'The Turquoise Cotinga.'

That Ford finally chose the name Edsel for the car was a crowning irony—especially in consideration of the fact that Edsel Ford—Henry Ford's son and the father of Henry Ford II—had been a man of impeccable taste.

Had he still been alive, the Edsel would certainly have been a different car. Edsel Ford had been the chief influence on Henry Ford to institute the styling department that produced the sleek Lincoln Continental of the late 1930s. If not for Edsel Ford, the Ford Motor Company would have drowned in a welter of basic, utilitarian designs. Therefore, the naming of the Edsel, an infamous styling

fiasco, may have him spinning in his grave even now.

The basic Edsel design was actually established in 1955, and all the dies and presses were set up for an attack on what was then projected to be a market hungry for extravagant styling. Unfortunately, 1957 was an aesthetic assault on the car buyer that effectively quenched popular taste for flashiness. The huge, shark-finned Cadillacs, Oldsmobiles, Buicks, Dodges and Chryslers of 1957 more than milked the market of whatever sentiment was left in favor of 'newness.'

Therefore, when the brand-new 1958 Edsel was introduced in the fall of 1957, there was a perceptible slump in auto sales. For model year 1958, Ford's share of the market went down from 1.7 million to 987,000; Pontiac went from 313,000 to

217,000; and Buick dropped from 404,000 to 241,000. The Edsel was an ugly duckling adrift upon a stormy sea.

For model year 1958, Edsel offered lower- and upper-range models. The lower-range models, designated Ranger and Pacer, had 352 cubic-inch (5.8-liter) engines, and were aimed at the Pontiac market. Edsel's upper-range Corsair and Citation models, with 410 cubic-inch (6.7-liter) engines, were meant to take customers from Buick and Oldsmobile.

The Ranger had a 118-inch (three-meter) wheelbase, and was available in two-door and four-door hardtop configurations. The Pacer was a slightly more plush version of the Ranger, and was offered in two- and four-door hardtop, as well as convertible, variants. Ranger and Pacer models were based on the Ford Fairlane 500 body shell.

The Corsair had a 124-inch (3.1-meter) wheelbase, and was available in two- and four-door hardtop versions. The Citation was the upscale version of the Corsair, with two- and four-door, as well as convertible, variants. Corsair and Citation models were based on the Mercury Parklane body shell.

There were also three station wagon models: Villager, Bermuda and Round Up, which looked just like the larger Fords of the same model year, but for the monstrous 'eat 'em alive' grillework.

The Villager and Bermuda wagons were available in standard and nine-passenger models, with the Round Up being strictly standard. All of the Edsels were large and heavy cars, with commonplace servo-assisted drum brakes, coil-spring independent front suspension and soft-leaf spring rear suspension with a conventional axle.

The cars were 'new' in such design details as the grillework and taillights, and in interesting—but often troublesome—gadgetry, including self-adjusting brakes, an electronically-operated transmission (on the upper-level cars) with selector buttons located in the hub of the steering wheel, electronic trunk opener and electrically-operated windows. For model year 1958, Edsel sold just 63,110 cars.

For 1959 Edsels, the headlights were faired into a horizontal grille that complemented the yawning mouth at the center, and reduced its impact to acceptable

Overleaf: A bright-red 1959 Edsel Corsair two-door hardtop. The Corsair was the only upper-level Edsel remaining that year. It was standardized with the lower-level Ranger on a 120-inch (three-meter) wheelbase. The Edsel was already a failure after just one year of sales.

Below: The front end of a 1958 Edsel Citation, evidencing the much-jeered Edsel 'horsecollar' grille. It was meant to evoke the tall and stately radiator grilles of the classic 1930s Packards, but was wildly out of context, and looked ridiculous.

(but still unforgettable) levels. The central grille was updated with prominent horizontal bars. The single-bar taillights were also replaced, with two straight lighting bars bearing two round red stop/turn signals and one round white backup light per side.

Also, the push-button transmission control was done away with; a six-cylinder engine was offered for the economy-minded, and the smaller V-8 was offered as standard on all models. The wheelbase of all non-station wagon models was standardized at 120 inches (3 meters), and only three models were offered: the Ranger, in two- and four-door variants; the Corsair, in two- and four-door, plus convertible, variants; and the Villager station wagon, in standard and nine-passenger configurations.

The auto industry perceived these cutbacks as tacit admission of failure, but a more concrete omen appeared at year's end: only 44,890 Edsels were sold.

The 1960 model year saw the first radical departure from the previous Edsel formula: the tragically distinctive grillework was replaced with a more standard, horizontal grille that somewhat resembled that of the upscale 1960 Mercurys and Fords. A centerpiece was laid in over this, which divided the grille into two areas that were shaped like bullets, nose-in toward the center.

The overall effect was like a 1960 Ford Galaxie. Only the Ranger—in two- and four-door, and convertible configurations—and the Villager station wagon—in six- and nine-passenger variants—were offered. Even at that, Ford Motor Company discontinued the Edsel before year's end, 1959, having built only 3008 of the 1960 model-year cars. There was a total of 111,009 Edsels built overall.

It is a historical irony that every Edsel that survives to today is a prized collector's item. In this small way, it could be said that the Edsel succeeded, albeit not

That the Edsel was a totally lost cause was evidenced by its final capitulation to conventional front-end design in 1960.

Standard Ford Motor Company components were used in the 1960 model-year cars, and there were to be no more Edsels after that. Below: A 1960 Edsel Ranger hardtop sedan.

in what it was intended for. Ford Motor Company lost between $250 and $350 million on the Edsel fiasco, setting a record for the costliest auto industry failure to that time.

Such a debacle might have been expected in a period of rapid change, as was the late 1950s. Jet aircraft had become commonplace, and mankind was already looking toward a new frontier. When the USSR orbited the first artificial satellite, *Sputnik*, on 4 October 1957, the world was stunned.

the market. Nothing much has improved, least of all this little smoke-belcher's thick contrail of bluish smoke. Trabants emit nine times more hydrocarbons and five times more carbon monoxide than the average Western car.

Environmental agencies from West Berlin and East Germany saw the chance to solve the problem, with the breaching of the infamous Berlin Wall in 1989. West Berlin suggested a maintenance tune-up program whereby Trabant emissions would be cut by perhaps 30 percent.

No less stunned were the nations of the captive Eastern Bloc, and they dutifully set about various projects to give honor to their tyrant 'protector' state.

1958–90 Trabant

East Germany's paean to *Sputnik* was a new car line, which was named Trabant, the German word for satellite. The Trabant was a small car with an inefficient, two-stroke engine that produced copious amounts of exhaust smoke and had a plastic body.

It was seen as the perfect car for the oppressed socialist country—cheap and crude. The problem is that the Trabants now being manufactured are almost identical to the Trabants of 30 years ago. As East Germany's primary automotive product, the Trabant has had a 'lock' on

However, with 2.2 million Trabants 'gassing it up,' the concept of fitting catalytic converters to these noxious little beasts would be more practical, as regular tune-ups of the cars' inefficient mechanisms could be a year-round task.

Then again, Volkswagen moved some of its operations into the main Trabant plant at Zwickau, West Germany in 1990, and plans are afoot for the production of a totally new Trabant. With that, the Trabant will cease being a Trabant—in other words, it will have lost its identity as a rich source of jokes.

Then again, perhaps not. One Trabant worker was heard to say that if the new Trabant has two tailpipes, it will make a fine wheelbarrow! Emblematic of the 'old' Trabant's torpid state is that the old Trabant Works' public relations director did not drive a Trabant—he rode a bicycle instead.

Above: *A Trabant. In 32 years of production, Trabant styling has not changed—nor has the terrible, smoke-belching Trabant engine.*

'Trabis,' as they are called by those who know and loath them, cannot conform to air-pollution limits of this or any time.

With East and West German reunification—and the concomitant availability of better cars for East Germans—Trabants are literally being abandoned. Soon, three million ownerless Trabants will litter the streets of 'the New Germany.'

Overleaf: *What may be considered to be an 'upper level' Trabant. Trabants have plastic bodies, and cannot be burned for fear of releasing toxic fumes into the atmosphere. Nor can they be easily recycled. In use or in waste, Trabants pose a major environmental problem.*

GRAND
ILLUSIONS

The economy wars had gone into full swing in the early 1960s, Renault had dropped off after its first year, and the homely but heartwarming Volkswagen was taking the lead. American automakers were not to be outdone by foreign competition in the economy car market, and their small car offerings were announced with dramatic publicity campaigns. Perhaps General Motors' offering had the most dramatic appeal of all—it was unlike any other American car.

1960–70 Chevrolet Corvair

As we have discussed earlier, the link between the automobile and the airplane is strong, and Ed Cole of Chevrolet's design department knew that. He dreamed of creating a car that would incorporate aircraft-like features for the benefit of all. In particular, he dreamed of a Chevrolet that would incorporate unit-body construction—an aircraft concept that was born out in several other American cars (including the Nash Airflyte) and a great many European autos.

Such a car, if sufficiently small, could utilize an air-cooled engine, which was another aircraft idea that had also been successfully exploited by such economy cars as the Volkswagen. Independent front and rear suspension, a distinctly European touch, would give the car smooth riding qualities, and would actually reduce production costs.

Such were the beginnings of the Chevrolet Corvair, a car begun with the best of intentions, but unable to live up to those intentions by dint of design flaws.

General Motors made a great show of pulling out all the stops, presenting a car with a sophisticated sort of European flair with a soapcake-like, boxy body that was thereafter emulated throughout the world by such auto makers as BMW.

The Corvair was powered by a 'pancake' six cylinder that, oddly, had bushings instead of main bearings, and was made of aluminum. The theory went that, with plenty of oil, the bushing would last as long as a bearing, but this was not so. These engines suffered early burnout when the main bushings wore down, and the aluminum block contributed to overheating.

Another liability was that the air-cooled 140-cubic-inch (2.3-liter) Corvair

six was a much larger engine than the tiny Volkswagen air-cooled four, and needed a very efficient air-ducting system to suit its cooling needs. That it lacked such was a shortcoming that was most apparent in the station wagon models.

The design of the Corvair wagon was at first considered a triumph. It seemed ingenious that Chevrolet could shoehorn a flat-six engine into a station wagon and still allow for rear cargo loading. Unfortunately, the design soon revealed the difficulty of routing cool air to the engine with a station wagon deck in the way. Therefore, overheating was a major problem.

Options on first-year Corvairs included a choice of three- or four-speed manual transmission, as well as a base-level two-speed automatic. Two engine options, 80

Opposite: *A 1960 Corvair Series 500 four-door sedan. This car represented the lowest trim level for the first Corvair production year, and was offered in two-and four-door variants—all with a six-person seating capacity.*

A higher trim level, the Series 700 cars, were offered with chrome exterior trim and various 'dressup' touches throughout.

The top of the line that first year was the Corvair Monza—essentially a Series 700 two-door with bucket seats and a sun roof.

The Corvair was the first mass-production, rear-engine, all-independent suspension American automobile. Unfortunately, the rear transaxle design was oversimplified— and that was the beginning of the Corvair's woes.

hp (on Standard and Deluxe models) or 95 hp (on Monza models), were also offered.

In keeping with the fashion of American cars in the 1950s–60s, the Corvair had four headlamps. All models, including the station wagon, were built on the same chassis.

The year 1961 saw the introduction of increased ranges for the Corvair, with each range connoting a level of comparative luxury. Beginning with the leanest accommodation, there was the Series 500, which offered a four-door sedan, a club coupe and a station wagon. Series 700 offered the same configurations, with more luxurious interiors and trim, and more options.

Above these were the Monza sedan and club coupe, sporting the widest range of options and performance options for the engine. Then there was the Greenbriar Sport Wagon, an upscale station wagon; and the Corvan, a small van available with or without side windows and removable extra seats.

The next year, 1962, saw the expansion of the Monza line to include a convertible and a station wagon; as well as the addition to the Corvair line of the Monza Spyder, which was designed to represent the very peak of Corvair performance. It featured a more powerful engine linked to a four-speed manual transmission. Among the Monza Spyder's performance options was a turbocharger.

This was also the year that Chevrolet installed a much stiffer handling package in the Corvair. There had been complaints that the car was a bit hard to han-

Previous pages: *A promotional still of a 1962 Corvair Monza convertible. Its 140-ci (2.3-liter) 'pancake' six-cylinder engine was offered in 80-hp and 95-hp versions. In 1964, more powerful, 140- and 180-hp, engines were offered for the sporty Corvair Corsa line.*

Even before the power increase, the Corvair was a dangerous automobile to drive. Please see the text.

dle. In wet conditions, or in turns at speed, the rear end wanted to break loose and swing around to the front, and the car suffered pronounced oversteer in general.

Complaints were also aired about the quality of Corvair interior trim. Even more serious complaints focused on the suspension design, and led Chevrolet to install a tranverse compensator spring. This was supposed to correct the rear wheels' tendency to tuck under at speed—which worsened the car's already skitterish handling.

The year 1964 saw much the same model lineup as 1963, except that Series 500 and 700 offerings were severely cut back to a club coupe and a sedan, respectively. General Motors launched the Corvair line even further into the performance market in 1965, offering the full Monza line as well as an even more performance-oriented car, the Corsa, in sport coupe and convertible variants.

Only the Greenbriar wagon, and Series 500 sedans and sport coupes, were offered for the lower range. The Corsa took over the performance edge from the Monza, offering 140- and 180-hp engines with which it could achieve 115 mph (185 kph).

The Corvair of 1965 was an overall superior, ostensibly safer car than had been the previous models, with wishbone rear suspension that vastly improved the handling and load-bearing of the car. Also, it had improved interior trim and a smoother, more flowing body style that was also more conventional.

Below: *A cutaway illustration of a pre-1965 Corvair design. It could be said that the post-1965 Corvairs were merely 'derived' from these earlier Corvairs.*

The later cars were, in fact, vastly superior, with Chevrolet having done all the structural work on them that they should have done on the originals.

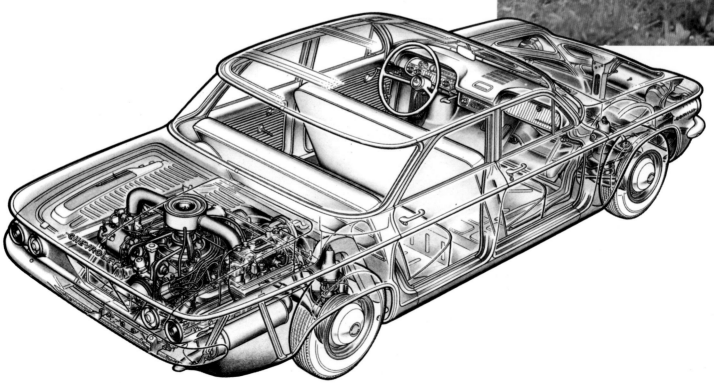

This same year, however, the crusading consumer advocate Ralph Nader released his book *Unsafe at Any Speed*. In it, he targeted General Motors' approach to vehicle safety, citing the Corvair as the prime example of design flaws for which the automaker should be held accountable for accidents suffered by General Motors products owners.

Nader stated that the worst flaw in pre-1965 Corvairs was their disastrous instability at highway speeds. This was due to several factors. The average Corvair had a standard curb weight of 2400 pounds (1091 kg), more than half of which was concentrated on the rear end of the car—against the better judgement of the Corvair's designer, Ed Cole.

With so much of the car's weight concentrated on it, the independent rear sus-

pension had to be built especially strong. As General Motors management dictated such cost-cutting measures as lightening the design, the suspension that the Corvair was built with was inadequate. It was a simple swing-axle setup, not much different than Edmund Rumpler's original design (please see the chapter 'They Might Have Been Great'), with little load-bearing support but the axles themselves, and *they* were too light to begin with. Thus, they tended to break when the car was at speed, and the car would go into an uncontrollable spin, sometimes flipping over entirely.

General Motors' directors confronted Ralph Nader in court, and the subsequent publicity only emphasized the points he had made in his book. *Unsafe at Any Speed* caused such a furor that

Above: *A 1966 Corvair Monza sport coupe.*

By the time this car was produced, the original Corvairs' accident record, and such public documents of same as Ralph Nader's exposé Unsafe at Any Speed, *had made the name 'Corvair' an anathema in American motoring.*

Strangely enough, Chevrolet's sales of its other lines were not really affected by the scandal.

Above: Curious onlookers surround an Amphicar. Essentially a car that also masqueraded as a boat, the Amphicar had a problem that was like a punchline to a bad joke for mariners: it tended to rust out.

Cruising down the highway, it made heads turn, with its pronounced boat-like profile. Many a following driver was nonplussed by the twin propellers that were tucked just under the Amphicar's rear bumper.

General Motors decided to let the Corvair program wind down.

For instance, 209,000 Corvairs were produced in 1965, but only 12,887 were produced in 1968. Previous to the *Unsafe At Any Speed* publicity, 1.5 million Corvairs had been sold, but afterward, sales accounted for only 125,000 Corvairs. Chevrolet announced the cancellation of the Corvair program in May of 1969.

The Corvair was by no means the most unusual car being touted in the 1960s. There was at least one that was almost on par with the McLaughlin Maine-mobile (see previous text) for versatility.

1961–65 Amphicar

The Amphicar was a West German-made convertible amphibian with Triumph components and a 14-foot (4.3-meter) hull. The body styling of this ver-

satile little sports car lay somewhere between that of a late-1960s Sunbeam Alpine and a Renault, with two nautical propellers at its rear. It was the result of 30 years of amphibious military vehicle research, as applied to a passenger car. Produced by the Quandt Group at Lubeck, West Germany, the 1961–65 Amphicar was then unique in being the only production amphibious passenger car in the world.

With its 70-cubic-inch (1.1-liter) Triumph four-cylinder engine, it could achieve up to 68 mph (109 kph) on the road, and eight mph (12.9 kph or seven knots) on water. Power was provided by a Triumph Herald four-cylinder engine. The front wheels functioned as rudders when the car was afloat.

During its years of import to the US, the Amphicar cost $3395, which was enough to buy a Chevrolet Biscayne and a boat and trailer—one of two reasons that the Amphicar was not a good buy.

The other, (and actually primary) reason was that the Amphicar was prone to rust—an extraordinarily bad problem in a vehicle that, above all, must be free of leaks. Once again, a more or less bright idea was snagged in mid-current—by an oversight of cataclysmic proportions.

Even Volkswagen, who had been successfully satisfying the popular taste for simplicity and economy with their ever-popular 'Beetle,' made mistakes. The company expanded the range of their offerings with the Squareback sedan, which was, for all intents and purposes, a two-door, rear-engine station wagon.

1966–75 Volkswagen Squareback

Introduced in 1966, these pleasant-looking little station wagons featured a 'pancake' 97.6-cubic-inch (1.6-liter),

dual-carburetor, four-cylinder engine of 65 hp. Squarebacks were the 'intermediate step' between Volkswagens of the 'beetle' and the Transporter varieties, and shared a 94.5-inch (2.4-meter) wheelbase with all Volkswagen offerings. The Squareback's overall length was 166.3 inches (4.2 meters)—just six inches longer than the 'Beetle.'

The Squareback was a good idea, as it allowed more room than the typically cramped confines of the beetle, yet it did not have the maneuvering drawbacks of the ungainly and underpowered Transporter micro-bus.

However, the Squareback suffered dreadfully from its 'pancake' four cylinder engine. This engine was designed to fit in the narrow space beneath the rear floor of the Squareback, and suffered from several mechanical inadequacies. Oil distribution was a problem, and—coupled with the near-impossibility of getting sufficient air into the cramped engine compartment for this air-cooled design—spelled disaster

Volkswagen resisted calling their Squareback sedan a station wagon, as they wanted to emphasize its sedan-like dimensions. They preferred calling it a 'squareback sedan.'

Be that as it may, it was, for all intents and purposes, a rear-engine station wagon, and the engine was squeezed into the shallow space below the rear cargo deck.

Its powerplant-cooling woes were like those of the Corvair station wagon (see text, this page and on page 106).

Overleaf: A Volkswagen Squareback sedan. The small louvers along the rear beltline were crucial to its engine-cooling system.

Below: *An Amphicar in use as a duck-hunting boat.*

At right: *Essentially the same as the Square-back, but with fastback styling, the Volkswagen Hatchback also shared the Squareback's troublesome rear-mounted, air-cooled, pancake-four engine format.*

both from premature bearing burnout and general overheating. These cars were carried as a line until 1975.

The next car under consideration had a completely different focus than that of the Squareback sedan. In fact, the car in question was built to be as striking and ostentatious as possible.

1967–75 Mohs

In 1967, the Mohs Seaplane Corporation of Madison, Wisconsin, elected to construct a series of truly unique cars. The first auto line that Mohs produced was a coupe, with Model A and B variants. These cars were loaded with exten-

sive and unusual special features, including sealed-beam taillights and a full-length steel rail built into each side of the car, for protection against broadside collisions.

The car's most unusual feature—apart from its massive chrome bumpers and monumental grillework—was its means of ingress and egress. While the BMW Isetta was tiny and had but a single, *front*-mounted door, the first Mohs car was huge and had only a single *rear*-mounted door, which swung up like a full-length hatchback.

This car—246 inches (6.2 meters) in overall length, with front and rear tread of 74 inches (1.8 meters)—was appropriately called the Ostentatienne Opera Sedan.

Model A cost $19,600 from the factory, and weighed 5470 pounds. It was powered by a 304-cubic-inch (4.9-liter) International Harvester V-8 truck engine, mated to a three-speed automatic transmission.

Model B had a factory price of $25,600, and weighed 6100 pounds. Its powerplant was a 250-horsepower, 549-cubic-inch (nine-liter) International Harvester V-8 truck engine, mated to a three-speed automatic.

The tires for these extravagant vehicles were mounted on 20-inch (51-cm) wheel-rims, and were inflated with nitrogen. Mohs body and trim style was an odd mixture of plain angularity and pipe-organ-like monumentality. This resulted in a bold, ugly and unforgettable visual impact.

In 1972, Mohs brought out a sports model. This was called the SafariKar, and had a retractable metal top. Its two doors slid open and closed on bushings mounted in longitudinal grooves along the sides of the car. Seating for eight was provided by jump seats, and the back seat converted into a bed large enough for two adults and two children.

The body had the typically shattering Mohs styling, and was made even more unusual by having an exterior composed of foam-padded Naugahide over aluminum.

Power was provided by a 179-horsepower, 392-cubic-inch (6.4-liter) International Harvester V-8 truck engine. The factory price for this 5400-pound (2450-kg), 240-inch-long (6.1-meter) convertible was $14,500.

Both the Ostentatienne Opera Sedan and the SafariKar were discontinued after model year 1975. The real wonder of these cars is that they were in production for as long as they were.

Opposite: *Uncompleted Mohs SafariKar convertibles, in both 'top down' and 'top up' modes. That the SafariKar's companion line was called the Ostentatienne Opera Sedan should come of no surprise after seeing these examples of gigantism in automobile styling.*

Note the laterally-sliding doors and the vinyl padded exterior. Seating for eight was provided by jump seats, and the back seat converted into a bed large enough for two adults and two children.

These 5400-pound, 240-inch-long (2450 kg, 6.1-meter) convertibles cost $14,500 from the factory.

THE FAILURE OF QUALITY CONTROL

Ralph Nader's *Unsafe at Any Speed* had made 'quality control' a part of popular rhetoric by the 1970s. It is strange, therefore, that the so-called 'era of quality control' was to produce some of the worst quality control fiascos the auto industry has ever seen. It seemed as if the attentions of government agencies and such 'crusaders' as Mr Nader prompted US automakers to produce cars *less* carefully.

This phenomenon did not apply solely to America, however. At the same time, several known and respected British and European firms were also producing defective cars that broke down and/or fell apart even as hapless consumers were still breaking them in.

There are no easy answers as to why or how this happened. Perhaps Western automakers became overconfident at having the market to themselves for so many years. Perhaps workers grew lax on the job, because of various and sundry conditions and factors. Certainly, the designs of some components were deficient, and some components that had been adequately designed failed by dint of poor construction.

Whatever the cause, the West was to pay dearly for its flaws, as the carbuying public turned slowly away from the automakers of the US, Great Britain and Europe, and very rapidly made the auto companies of Japan wealthy by buying more and more of *their* cars.

Indeed, the automakers of Japan— Honda, Toyota, Datsun and Subaru— who had once turned out rather retrograde vehicles, had gotten the knack of producing well-made cars that had great appeal to Western buyers. These cars included the epochal Datsun 240Z— which proved that the Japanese were capable of far more than the tinny 'econo-boxes' that they had produced in the 1960s—and the renowned Toyota Corollas of the late 1970s. Then again, there were the early Mazda rotary-car disasters (please see).

While Western automakers have improved dramatically from those nightmarish days of the 1970s, the Japanese are now apparently 'here to stay' as a major competitive force.

1969–76 Fiat

Normally well-built cars that gave sportscar-like performance on the highway, Fiat models 850, 124, 126, 127 and 128 for the model years 1969 to 1976 suffered severe rust and corrosion problems. In the US and Canada, these Fiats seemed

Fiat had a solid reputation as a builder of small cars. Then came the era of bad quality control, which was a Euro-American epidemic in the early 1970s.

In Fiat's case, the years 1969–76 bode ill for Fiat models 850, 124, 126, 127 and 128: these cars seemed to self-destruct in a cloud of rust even as their new owners watched.

This was especially the case with cars that had been exported to North American climes. Below: An early-1970s Fiat Model 850 coupe.

to disintegrate before their owners' eyes, as massive amounts of rust and corrosion overwhelmed both bodies and undercarriages. Severe chassis corrosion was also endemic to Fiats in Europe.

The US government sued Fiat for failing to recall 133,500 severely rusting 1970–71 850 models. While this was but a drop in the proverbial bucket, it was one up on the Canadian government's deal with Fiat Canada to recall and rustproof their rapidly oxidizing Fiats. Even with the recall

was to come from Sweden, where Volvo had long established a reputation for building extremely reliable and durable automobiles.

1970–76 Volvo

Something happened in 1970, and this something continued to happen through the year 1976, in the assembly lines of

and rustproofing, deterioration recommenced, unabated.

Suspension and steering problems, caused by corrosion, were also among the defects making 1969–76 Fiat owners miserable. Frequent engine and clutch breakdowns further plagued these cars. With model year 1977, Fiat had the rust problem in abatement, in contrast to the 1969–76 models that practically rusted to dust before their owners' horror-stricken eyes. It was a shame, as Fiat's handily-sized little cars (with wheelbases of about 90 inches or 2.3 meters) might have had garnered a greater market share but for the above-mentioned problems.

The failure of the Fiat line was bad enough, but one of the biggest shocks

Sweden's Volvo. Those who had bought and relied upon Volvos suddenly found that the new Volvos were defective, with rust making itself known within the first year of ownership.

Bad wheel bearings, fuses, carburetors, alternators, regulators, clutches, internal engine parts, locks, radios and windows were among the ailments encountered with the full range of Volvos from these years. If mechanical difficulties in and of themselves weren't enough, drivers reported bizarre performance patterns that caused some Volvo owners to state that their cars drove so erratically that they appeared to be 'possessed.'

Gas guzzling and oil burning added to

Above: A Fiat 127 coupe. Early 1970s Fiat bodies survived a bit better in their home climate of Italy—altogether, a more benign set of environmental conditions than are found in most of North America, where the little cars practically disintegrated.

Above: A 1970 Volvo 144 sedan. Volvo had established a strong reputation as a builder of durable, reliable, high-quality automobiles.

In the early 1970s, it seemed that Volvo would be the least likely of all automakers to have quality control problems. Unfortunately, Volvos of the years 1970–76 were riddled with quality-control-originated flaws (please see text).

Previous pages: A 1974 Volvo 164 sedan.

Everything from paint finish to basic mechanical systems was prone to failure. It was all part of the quality-control illness that was, as we shall see, pandemic among western automakers in the early 1970s.

the list of complaints. Many drivers had difficulty starting their cars in hot *or* cold weather. Volvo issued a 'Cold-Start Kit' to help with these woes. Additionally, Volvo recalled its 1975 and 1976 164, 240 and 260 model cars for gas-fume seepage into the passenger compartment.

Volvos of later and earlier years are considered to be good cars, but, as with Ford and its Edsel, everyone makes mistakes. Volvos of the 1970–76 period were offered in four-door sedan, two-door sedan, coupe and station wagon models on wheelbases graduating from 96.5 to 107.1 inches (2.4 to 2.7 meters).

One of the biggest automotive mistakes of the 1970s caused a furor that rivalled Ralph Nader's expose of the Corvair—and like *that* controversy, was generated by an American automaker. The car in question seemed to be a timely design—simple, inexpensive and with a modicum of aesthetic appeal.

1970–76 Ford Pinto

The Pinto was Ford's attempt at a subcompact car, and with a 94.2-inch (2.3-meter) wheelbase, it seemed suited to the role. However, the running gear of the Pinto was not a strong suit. It was seriously underpowered with its standard four-cylinder which, coupled with an astonishingly puny automatic transmission, produced a car that seemed to have the motive power of a wet sponge.

Even the last year produced, the 1976 Pinto, had an automatic transmission that habitually slipped from park to reverse—not a comforting thought, given the Pinto's *major* flaw, which we'll discuss shortly.

The Pinto's bulging sides, sloping back and insensibly long hood seemed to come from several disparate designs, but was intended to give this small, light car the appearance of elegance and forward motion. Indeed, some found that they liked the little car on the basis that it 'looked friendly.'

The most dismal aspect of the Pinto was its propensity to explode in a ball of flame when hit from behind. That even a moderate 'fender-bender' could result in death by fire is a numbing fact that hangs over the 1970–76 Pinto like the shadow of the Grim Reaper. Ford Motor Company did take steps, after being sued, to correct the problem by a massive recall campaign. The explosion problem was due, after all, to a defect in the gas tank ventilation system.

Steps were taken to correct many of the problems we have discussed in later editions of the Pinto, but some persisted into the late 1970s.

Thanks to the long-standing convention of developing parallel vehicle lines, the slightly more upscale Mercury Comets of 1970–76 suffered the same woes as their Pinto brethren.

By the laws of automotive competition, General Motors had to produce cars that were competitive with the Ford Motor Company products. Therefore, Chevrolet brought out its notorious Vega line. The mystery is why this small car was nearly as bad as its Pinto competitor—an informative coincidence, altogether.

Overleaf: A 1976 Pinto runabout, representative of the last year the benighted Pinto was produced.

Ford packed a lot of trouble into the subcompact Pinto (see text). With a wheelbase of 94.2 inches (2.3 meters), and a choice of either a 97.6-ci (1.6-liter) or a 122-ci (two-liter) four-cylinder engine, the Pinto seemed like a winner when it was introduced in 1971.

Even though the Pinto looked good on paper, it just didn't work out on the road.

Transmission problems and engine problems added to the little car's woes. Worst of all was its tendency to explode when struck from behind.

At left and below: A 1974 Pinto runabout. This was the year that energy-absorbing bumpers were added to the little car, giving it a more substantial appearance.

1971–75
Chevrolet Vega

Better styled than the Pinto, the Vega's comparatively large slotted wheels appeared to the casual observer to be spoked, and therefore evoked cars of that happier, simpler time when General Motors founder WC Durant battled Henry Ford, and both contributed to the betterment of public motoring. In fact, the Vega looked a little sassy as well.

These little cars were offered in sedan and station wagon models, on a 97-inch (2.4-meter) wheelbase for the period

The body tended to rust as if a rust *blitzkreig* were unleashed: it rusted everywhere, with daunting rapidity. Just a few months after first purchase, the car acquired a patina of bubbles which soon burst reddish-brown through the finish.

The four-cylinder engine was made of aluminum, and its design hadn't been fully worked out. Therefore, this powerplant quite often developed warped cylinder heads, various and sundry leakage problems, oil burning (from extreme expansion and contraction of cylinder walls) and main bearing failure.

Throttle linkage also tended to kink, producing full power at inopportune moments. Many Vegas also had steering

Above: *Meant as an all-new sub-compact car, the Vega, like the Ford Pinto, was built by a company that had never built a sub-compact before.*

Therefore, the Vega project represented untried territory for Chevrolet—and in the era of poor quality control, that meant disaster.

The Pontiac Astre, inaugurated in 1975, was Vega's late-blooming 'sister line,' and shared many of the Vega woes.

from 1971–75. That the Vega was an economy car was somewhat belied by its erratic fuel consumption, which, for the first year of production, gave a fair 23 mpg (37 kpg). This dipped to an abysmal 13 mpg (21 kpg) in the year 1973 (as tallied with a standard, four-cylinder model), and rose again to 20 mpg (32 kpg) for the year 1975. By contrast, the Vega's weight rose steadily from 2200 to 2495 pounds (1000 to 1134 kg) through the same years.

In terms of passenger access, Vegas were difficult to enter and exit, and many remember snagging a pocket, lapel or handbag as they twisted up and away upon egressing from the car. The illusion of spunkiness was shattered with the turn of a key. The car was equipped with a mushbox automatic transmission, or a trauma-producing mess that passed for a standard transmission. Neither transmission had the grace to refrain from outright breakdown, even though mated to an insipid four-cylinder engine.

and brake problems. On the 1972–73 models, rear axles were among the leading problem areas, and for the 1971–75 range, drive train problems in general were rife.

While steps were taken to correct defects on post-1975 models, General Motors dropped this line after 1977.

The slightly more upscale Pontiac Astre was General Motors' parallel line for the Vega, and followed the Vega in General Motors production by four years. Astres of 1975 suffered many of the same defects as their Vega brethren.

As we shall see, the West was not the sole victim of quality-control breakdown. Among the early Japanese cars to be imported to the West in quantity were a host of small, doubtful-looking vehicles that barely qualified as what most Westerners would have called 'cars.' They were practically cycle-cars.

These were the oriental equivalent of the 'bubble cars' (see the text on the

Above and left: *This 1974 Vega hatchback coupe is still running, but when the doors are opened and shut, rust sifts through the headliner, and showers the car's interior.*

This merely underscores one of many problems encountered with this rather nice-looking little car.

In 1975, Chevrolet offered a limited-edition Vega called the Cosworth Vega, which featured a dual-overhead cam, 16-valve, four-cylinder Cosworth racing engine. It didn't serve to redeem the contemporaneous standard Vegas, but it surely surprised the unsuspecting.

BMW Isetta) that some Western manufacturers produced in the wake of World War II.

In fact, many of these little cars—the Hondas, Datsuns and Toyotas of the 1960s—were little more than greatly-minimalized versions of obsolete Western car designs. Mechanical quality was marginal, quality control was doubtful and passenger comfort was often nonapplicable. The main appeal of these little cars was their fuel economy.

As Japan began to gain on the West, and sales increased, Japanese automakers plowed their profits into improving their products, and fearlessly copied whenever they could, placing emphasis on quality rather than originality. Hence, by the mid-1970s, Toyota, Datsun and several other makes had staked a substantial and increasing claim on Western markets.

Some of these cars, however, caused more of a wry grin than an approving nod from their prospective Western customers. Some of them were highly flawed, and some merely looked weird. Probably the most famous Japanese fail-

ure in the foreign marketplace involved the early Mazda rotary-engine design, which is discussed in our chapter entitled 'They Might Have Been Great.' There were others, too.

Pre-1971 Subaru

The pre-1971 Subarus were egg-shaped little cars. Subaru's eccentric approach to design was never more evident than in these tinny little creations that seemed to have popped out of only slightly-larger-than-life gum-ball machines.

A relatively progressive example of these early Subaru import offerings was the Star, in two- and four-door sedan and four-door wagon variants, with a 95.2-inch (2.4-meter) wheelbase.

Essentially, the late-1960s Subarus were motorcycles with an extra pair of wheels, and an enlarged, enclosed passenger compartment. Fittings were shoddy, engine noise was of aircraft volume, and failure of mechanical systems was commonplace.

Below: A 1971 Subaru Model 1100 sedan. The 1100 was the sister line to the egg-shaped Subaru 360.

The upscale 1100 at least looked somewhat like a conventional car, but was still in step with the 'cycle cars' that are discussed in the third chapter of this book.

Extremely light-gauge metalwork promoted early corrosion and rusting, not to mention the demise of such under-strengthened features as bumpers and chrome tailpipe tips.

With tiny wheels and small passenger compartments, these cars were not built to travel far—nor even to get across a moderately large city. Exterior paint schemes ran a gamut of colors that seemed inspired by neon signs.

Later models improved dramatically, and by the mid-1970s, Subaru had one of the best repair records in the auto industry.

To combat the influx of imports, automakers in the US not only brought out such models such as the Pinto and the Vega—they also changed their large-car lines by replacing older models with brand-new ones. This did not always succeed.

1971–77 Ford Torino

The 1971 Torino was Ford's replacement of its dependable mid-sized Fairlane. With a 118-inch (three-meter) wheelbase, and weighing in at 3700 to 4259 pounds (1682 to 1936 kg) (increasing with the years of production), the Torino was on the heavy side of the 'mid-size' equation.

The obvious trouble with the Torino was that its body styling contributed to the pooling of water on surfaces, encouraging a pervasive rust problem. In fact, it had a reputation as a 'biodegradable car,' due to its tendency to rust rapidly and over large body areas—a tendency that was exacerbated by a paint job that was prone to peeling.

Economy was the word among Ameri-

Above: *A 1971 Subaru Model 360 coupe. Subaru seemed to be normalizing its auto styling with the Subarus of 1971.*

Even so, the tiny Model 360, with a gross weight of 925 pounds, was basically a four-wheel motorcycle.

Opposite: *A 1971 Ford Torino GT coupe. The expansive, flat body surfaces that Ford favored for their Torinos promoted the pooling of water on body surfaces, and hence the formation of rust.*

These cars were plagued by mechanical and other woes.

Below: *A 1975 Gran Torino coupe. While the 1968 Torinos had a rather ungainly look with their huge fastback roofs, later Torinos had excesses of flat body planes.*

The mechanical woes began with the 1971 model year.

can automakers of the early 1970s, and in some cases, efforts were made to create a car that would appeal to two or more groups—for instance, families and 'muscle car' lovers. Rambler had futilely attempted such a feat with their Marlin 'sports sedan' of 1965–67. Aesthetically, the first Torino was very much like the Marlin, having a boxy variety of 'family car' styling, with the addition of a fastback of the sort usually associated with sports models. The Torino was still officially a Fairlane, and would be until 1970.

As the years went on, its window design afforded the driver a poor view of the immediate surroundings.

Brakes, transmission and suspension problems added to post-1970 Torino's woes, and the tendency of wheel bearings to wear out rapidly was a pronounced safety problem. While the basic six-cylinder powerplant was dependable, it did not provide adequate power for the

rather heavy car it had to haul, and many owners found that these engines lost a lot of power due to faulty spark advance/delay mechanisms.

Carburetor, fuel line and power steering problems occurred on the 1973 models as well. Torino automatic transmissions tended to slip from park to reverse, and the differentials of these cars frequently broke down.

The suspension and brake problems seemed to have been cured by 1974, but with this model year, the six-cylinder had been replaced as the standard engine by a 351 cubic-inch (5.8-liter) V-8. With this engine, the power problem for the basic Torino was solved, but reports of cracked engine blocks abounded. Rusting, as ever, persisted. The electrical system also became a problem.

The 1975 Torino had engine, transmission, brake and carburetor problems, as well as the all-too-familiar body defects.

These pages: *A 1972 Mercury Montego, rep-*
resentative of the Torino's 'sister line' that
shared many of the Torino's problems. Note
the strange flatness of this car's hood: envi-
sion a large puddle of water pooling on its
expansive surface.

   This car greatly resembled the 1972 Ford
Torino, and was not alone in that—such like-
nesses were industry-wide, which led to a
certain anonymity among early-1970s Ameri-
can cars.

The 1976 Torino still had a few 'bugs,' but not quite as many as the previous model years. Almost ironically, Ford Motor Company had at last decided to terminate the Torino from the FoMoCo production schedule, and 1977 saw the last—and probably the best—Torinos roll off the assembly line.

The slightly more upscale Mercury Montego of 1972–76 was a parallel model to the Torino, and suffered woes that were similar to those suffered by the Torino.

While American automakers fought the economy wars, some of their peers tried to resurrect the grand old ideas of the past, such as the flying car. Perhaps its was felt that, with an economy war going on, the ultimate trump of all competition would be a vehicle that was not only an economical *car*, but an economical *airplane* as well.

Above: *An illustration of a 1973 Aircar. The Aircar was a 1973 Ford Pinto with flying components from a Cessna Skymaster.*

The project ended when the Aircar crashed during a test flight. Perhaps it's just as well, considering the Pinto's history on the ground.

1973 Aircar

The Aircar was yet one more attempt to develop an economical car for the driver who finds the average highway a bit too confining.

As a commercial venture, the Aircar had an extra burden to overcome, however: the automobile component was a 1973 Ford Pinto, one of the most notorious cars of the 1970s (please see the text on same).

Mated to this 94.2-inch-long (2.3-meter) Pinto 'fuselage' were the modified wings and stabilizers of a Cessna Skymaster airplane.

A structural failure caused the Aircar to crash during a test flight in 1973. The development program for this flight-capable automobile was terminated shortly after this accident.

Even such a bold attempt to part with the ground was a mere footnote compared to the ongoing automobile economy wars, which were complicated by rampant poor quality control.

1973–76 Volkswagen Dasher

The Dasher of 1973–76 was presented in two- and four-door sedan models, plus a station wagon and a hatchback model (in 1976), on a 97.2-inch (2.4-meter) wheelbase. This was a Volkswagen 1970s trouble machine. In general, Dashers dashed many bank accounts—as they had abnormally high repair rates on brakes and engines.

Dasher water-cooled engines were a new twist for Volkswagen—used as that company was to air-cooled designs. Perhaps the design was too new: Dasher engines tended to overheat. The Dasher foreshadowed the ills of the 1975–76 Volkswagen Rabbit, which also caused many woes (please see text on same).

Post-1976 Dashers surmounted the above-cited obstacles, and the line was expanded in the late 1970s.

To the dismay of car buffs worldwide, British Leyland Motors was suffering its share of quality-control woes at this time, too.

Above: *A 1974 Dasher two-door sedan. Dashers were among the first front-engine, water-cooled Volkswagens.*

Dashers were received enthusiastically, but it soon became clear that the Volkswagen company had not worked out all the 'bugs.'

Built on a nimble 97.2-inch (2.4-meter) wheelbase, there was much promise, but a lot of trouble with the pre-1976 Dashers.

At left: *A 1975 Dasher four-door sedan (background) and a 1975 Dasher two-door hatchback.*

Volkswagen stayed with the line, and eventually worked through the problems. Post-1976 Dashers were much improved over their predecessors.

1973–75 Austin Marina

Below: *A 1974 Marina GT coupe. The Marina, a small car with a wheelbase of 96 inches (2.4 meters), was made in several models, including two- and four-door sedans, and included a GT version.*

Below, at bottom: *A 1974 Marina four-door sedan. Electrical systems failures, fuel leaks, front-end vibration and a monstrous amount of oversteer were among 1973–75 Marina problems—and a bizarre flaw lay in the transmission (see text).*

The 1973–75 Austin Marinas were among British Leyland's cavalcade of mid-1970s lemons (see also 1974–78 Triumph and 1975–76 Jaguar models). In four-door sedan and two-door 'GT Coupe' models, these little four-cylinder cars had a standard wheelbase of 96 inches (2.4 meters).

The 1973–75 Austin Marinas almost without exception exhibited severe front-end vibration at speeds between 55 and 65 mph (88 and 104 kph). This vibration

generally occurred after 5000 miles (8045 km) had been put on the cars. It resulted from a very bad, flimsily-designed steering and suspension apparatus. This also resulted in persistent cupping—uneven wear—of the tires. Repeated alignments and wheel balancings did nothing to cure this problem.

Windshield wiper/washer failures, horn failures, panel-light failures and persistent fuse burnouts resulting from badly-designed wiring arrangements also afflicted these cars. The 1974 Marinas, in particular, suffered from defective gasoline filler pipes that leaked fuel into their

luggage compartments; and numerous fuel leaks occurred in Marina engine compartments.

Stalling in traffic was a problem that was traceable to one of two sources: a defective gas pedal cable, which tended to break under normal usage; and/or a badly-designed carburetor.

Last, but certainly not least, there was a major transmission problem. Occasionally, when Austin Marina drivers tried to engage first or reverse gear in the car, the transmission would engage *both* first and reverse simultaneously, destroying itself.

Some Japanese automakers were also having quality-control problems.

1973–75 Honda Civic

The Honda Civics of 1973–75 were powered by four-cylinder engines, and were offered in sedan, hatchback sedan and four-door station wagon models (in 1975)—all on a 86.6-inch (2.2-meter) wheelbase.

Above: *A 1973 Austin Marina GT coupe. In 1952, Austin merged with the Morris firm (which itself controlled the MG, Wolseley and Riley automaking firms) to form British Motor Corporation, which was subsequently merged with Leyland Motors to form British Leyland in 1968.*

Some of the Austin and Morris cars were essentially the same. Thus it was that the mid-1970s Morris Marinas suffered the same flaws as the Austin Marinas.

The basic Honda Civic body style has not changed much over the years. However, as the text points out, what matters most is what the body shell contains.

Above: A 1974 Honda Civic. Much-touted imports, 1973–75 Honda Civics were made in sedan and station wagon models. They would have been good little economy cars, except that they repeatedly broke down.

Honda did, in fact, redeem the Honda Civic's name with later, mechanically superior, renditions of the basic design.

At first heralded as a dream car for those seeking an affordable and versatile automobile, the Honda Civic turned into a nightmare for many auto owners. Brakes, engines and transmissions were the centers of failure for the 1973–75 Hondas. Carburetor problems also abounded.

Aside from the safety factor of bad brakes, the engine and transmission problems were especially onerous, as these were, after all, front-wheel-drive automobiles. Therefore, if work on an engine necessitated its being 'pulled,' the entire drive train had to come out.

Likewise, any work on the transmission carried the same onus. While that is true of any front-wheel-drive car, the 1973–75 Honda Civics needed such work too often to qualify them as the 'economy cars' that they were built to be.

It took time, but Honda's quality-control ills were all but forgotten by the late 1970s, even though Toyota had by then outstripped Honda as the Japanese make to buy in the West.

Meanwhile, the 1970s had begun to turn into a bad dream for British Leyland, with one after another of their famous makes suffering from epidemic defects.

1974–78 Triumph

The Triumph TR-1s, TR-2s and TR-3s of the 1950s and 1960s were 'everyman's sportscars,' and while they required 'getting out and under' to fix their various quirks from time to time, that was an understood and accepted part of owning a sportscar at the time.

However, as British Leyland advanced the Triumph line toward more powerful cars with farther-reaching capabilities, they seemed to leave the solid ground of mechanical care that they had taken with the cantankerous, but understandable, earlier models. What arose in the mid-1970s was a deplorable run of outright faulty manufacture and bad design ideas. There was a severe problem with quality control that had in fact been building since the late 1960s.

The lowest point of quality control was reached in the Triumph model years from 1974–78. These cars included Spitfire, Spitfire 1500, TR-6 and TR-7 models, with convertible and hardtop variants. Spitfires and Spitfire 1500s had 83-inch (2.1-meter) wheelbases, TR-6s had 88-inch (2.2-meter) wheelbases and TR-7s had 85-inch (2.1-meter) wheelbases. Spitfires and TR-7s of 1974–78 were powered by four-cylinder engines, while TR-6s had six-cylinder powerplants.

Ignition amplifier failures were a common cause of in-traffic stalling for these Triumphs, and outright loss of power due to breakage-prone gas pedal cables were real drawbacks on the TR-7 models. On the other hand, 1974 TR-6s had accelerator linkage problems that all too often led to uncontrolled acceleration.

Early TR-7s had rear-axle suspension linkage that was defective, and seriously affected driver control of the car. Additionally, TR-250 and TR-6 models from as early as 1968 to 1976 had a defective lower trunion pin that was designed without an obligatory grease fitting. This pin, an integral part of the vehicle's steering apparatus, was known to break on rough roads, or when crossing over railroad tracks.

Also, these same models had defective brake proportioning valves that occasionally blew the dashboard warning light completely out of its socket—and only then would the warning light flash on, telling the driver that his brakes were *in danger of failing* when they had *already* failed.

Engine fires were a problem for the 1975 Spitfires, and 1974 TR-5 models had the unfortunate potential for fuel leaks from a number of defective sources in the engine compartment.

Windshield wiper/washer failures, horn failures, panel light failures and persistent fuse burnouts resulted from badly-designed wiring arrangements in 1974–78 Triumphs. This litany of problems was only part of a mounting disaster for one of the world's great automakers.

Overleaf: *A 1977 Triumph Spitfire 1500. Triumph was another segment of British Leyland (see also the commentary on the 1973–75 Austin Marina) that was severely affected by poor quality control.*

The cars so affected were the Triumph Spitfire, Spitfire 1500, TR-6 and TR-7 of the years 1974–78.

Below: *A 1974 Triumph TR-6.*

Below, at bottom: *A 1975 Triumph TR-7, with the wedge profile that was promoted as 'the shape of the future.'*

Electrical and mechanical problems blunted this car's cutting edge in the marketplace.

On the other side of the Atlantic, American Motors Corporation created a new model that was a sensation when it first came out, but quickly lost its appeal.

1975–80 AMC Pacer

This unusual, gumdrop-shaped little car was originally designed for a rotary engine (see also, the text sections on the NSU Spider and Ro80, as well as the 1970–

Below: *A 1975 Pacer sedan. The Pacer, with its 171.5-inch (4.4-meter) overall length, offered as much interior room as larger cars. Designed conveniently with an extra-long curb-side door, for easy exit and entry, it seemed destined for success.*

Bad quality control, plus a last-minute engine substitution, helped to ultimately defeat the Pacer in the marketplace.

73 Mazda models), but AMC's plans for the rotary were scrapped, and an underpowered six-cylinder was substituted. At first, this was a 232-cubic-inch (3.8-liter) powerplant, but the displacement was increased, with little effect, to 258 cubic inches (4.2 liters) in 1979.

For an economy car, the Pacer delivered terrible gas mileage, never rising above the 14–15 mpg (23–24 kpg) range in all its years of production, even though the tortoise-like body was mounted on a compact, 100-inch (2.5-meter) wheelbase.

The 1975–80 AMC Pacer had electrical and carburetor glitches that caused stalling and other power plant problems, as well as door frames that were prone to

rust. The steering, especially on the 1976 models, has been known to seize—a serious safety defect. Brake defects began to make themselves known after the first year, and a defective lower control arm further added to this car's steering assembly woes.

Vibrations and rattles, plus poor interior finish and bad body panel fitting further dampened the aesthetic appeal of this already rather startling-looking little car. Electrical system bugs were worked out in the last two years (1979 and 1980) of production, and the engine was replaced with a larger but ineffective power plant.

An easy-to-pick rear hatch lock was but further evidence that this attempted economy car was a *futile* attempt by a premier maker of economy cars.

Other automakers faced other problems in that age of corporate stumbling. Perhaps it was the radical change from predominately rear-engine designs to front-engine, front-wheel-drive designs that gave rise to many of Volkswagen's troubles in the 1970s.

1975–76 Volkswagen Rabbit

While the Volkswagen 'beetle' was beloved by its owners, its successors in Volkswagen's bid to become the premier small car manufacturer in the Western world were not so adored. In particular, the Volkswagen Rabbit of 1975–76 (see also the previous text on the Dasher) suffered greatly in its maiden years. Rabbits in these years were offered in a number of configurations, including two- and four-door hatchback sedans, with custom and deluxe variations, all on a 94.5-inch (2.4-meter) wheelbase.

Brakes, exhaust, engine and cooling system problems were major contributors to the Rabbit's ills, while a veritable tumult of squeaks and rattles from poor fit and trim added to Rabbit drivers' woes.

Particularly, engine seizure due to bad lubrication was a problem, and excessive smoke from the diesel models was an irritating and often embarassing occurrence. Many a Rabbit owner found his less-than-one-year-old diesel Rabbit belching black plumes of exhaust from its tailpipe. Both diesel and gasoline engines were known to fail in such a manner that great expense was required to fix them.

Additionally, diesel models sometimes

Above: *A mid-1970s Volkswagen Scirocco. Due to its close relationship to the Rabbit, the 1975–76 Scirocco shared many of the mid-1970s Rabbit defects.*

It was an upscale 'econobox,' but engine problems and other quality-control defects greatly lessened its appeal.

At left: *Two 1975 Volkswagen Rabbit hatchback sedans, in two- and four-door configurations.*

The 'hatchback' was one of the hottest gimmicks in mid-1970s automaking circles, as it allowed easy access to cargo space.

Rabbit diesels of 1975–76 were the most flagrantly difficult cars of the Rabbit line of the mid-1970s, as they tended to belch smoke after a year of use.

had a tendency to suddenly and mysteriously accelerate for 10 to 15 seconds, with no relation to the actual position of the throttle linkage.

Cylinder heads, oil leaks, crankshaft breakage and bad fuel pumps were still other woes that Rabbit owners of these model years faced. In some cases, freakish engine oil pressure resulted in cracked oil filters. In other cases, the oil filters were literally blown off the engines by abnormal oil pressure.

The number-one repair remedy for gasoline-engine Rabbits of 1975–76 was a complete engine replacement. Additionally, brake master cylinder failure was a disastrous possibility for all Rabbits. In general, the Volkswagen Rabbit of 1975–76 was not a good car. Rabbits of later model years showed vast improvement.

In keeping with the rules of parallel development adhered to by many modern automakers, contemporaneous lines tended to share virtues and defects. Just so, the Volkswagen Scirocco of 1975–76 shared the defects of the 1975–76 Volkswagen Rabbit.

Meanwhile, not only were British Leyland's popular Triumph and Austin Marina models suffering from manufacturing defects, so, too, was their flagship line, the renowned Jaguar.

1975–76 Jaguar

Jaguars of 1975–76 were offered on 108.8- and 113-inch (2.7- and 2.8-meter) wheelbases, in two-door coupe and four-door sedan variants, with model designations XJ6, XJ6-L, XJ6-C, XJ12, XJ12-L and XJ12-C, to signify six- or 12-cylinder models with coupe or long wheelbase.

Below: *A 1975 Jaguar XJ6 sedan—a sleek and sophisticated car that was ruined by poor quality control. The damage was more or less contained to 1975–76, when poorly designed electrical systems and a tendency to stall while in motion created unacceptable risks for car owners.*

Both six- and 12-cylinder 1975–76 Jaguar models suffered from stalling while in motion. This serious defect had implications for any road condition or situation—from passing other cars on a highway to taking a peaceful country drive.

This was at least in part due to the fact that the ignition amplifier that was commonly installed in these cars was not capable of functioning in weather that was warmer than 90 degrees, and, additionally, aged prematurely.

Defective fuel pumps were another much-decried source of engine stalling in the 1975–76 Jaguars, and the crossover switch that accessed the fuel in the reserve fuel tanks that these cars had was another source of breakdown.

Some Jaguars of 1975–76 also had defective power steering, in which the fluid sump leaked. Faulty disc brakes and a faulty remote-control door latching sys-

tem also added up to disaster if emergency situations arose. Windshield wiper/washer failures, horn failures, panel light failures and persistent fuse burnouts resulting from badly-designed wiring arrangements further added to the list of common defects on these cars.

American automakers, not to be outdone, also continued to manifest fresh quality-control and design disasters. For instance, Chrysler Corporation followed a similar path to that taken by Ford's Torino.

1977–80 Dodge Aspen

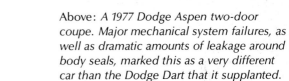

Above: *A 1977 Dodge Aspen two-door coupe. Major mechanical system failures, as well as dramatic amounts of leakage around body seals, marked this as a very different car than the Dodge Dart that it supplanted.*

What a difference a year makes! In 1977, the venerable Dodge Dart and its sister model, the Plymouth Valiant, were renamed Aspen and Volare, respectively.

While formerly afflicted with faulty interior seals along the front door posts, the new, renamed cars seemed to have been subtly redesigned to provide for increased drainage into the interior, adding a trunk leakage problem as well. Also, the front fenders of these cars were prone to rapid rusting—there was a company compensation policy, begun in 1976, of free fender replacement.

Armed with a standard 225-cubic-inch (3.7-liter) six cylinder, Aspens and Volares managed a best fuel economy of 18 mpg (29 kpg), and an absolutely abysmal worst of 13 mpg (20 kpg) for the model year 1978. The wheelbase for the 1977 Aspen/Volare was 115 inches (2.9 meters), cut down to 108.7 inches (2.7 meters) for 1978 and 1979, and increasing to 112.7 inches (2.8 meters) for 1980.

Starting motor and transmission failures plagued the first year of the Aspen/

Above: A 1980 Plymouth Volare. Wheel-bearing seizures, electrical system failures and differential breakdowns were among the woes that afflicted these cars.

This was the last year for the Volare and its sister make, the Dodge Aspen—both victims of the quality-control plague of the 1970s.

Below: A 1980 Oldsmobile Ninety-Eight Regency sedan—in itself elegant and substantial, but when equipped with the General Motors 350-ci (5.7-liter) diesel V-8, it was a disaster.

Unfortunately, the 350-ci (5.7-liter) diesel was merely a redesigned gasoline engine, and was incapable of maintaining the pressures of diesel operation.

Volare. As the decade played itself out, this model line only got worse. While the Dart and Valiant were accounted among the best American economy cars for much of their market lives (which began in 1960), their successors seemed to plunge straight downhill in terms of reliability and quality.

Major engine and transmission problems appeared with increasing frequency as the production years rolled on. Aspens and Volares uniformly had chronic stalling problems, and the brakes were faulty on many of them. The front suspension pivot bar was prone to break, and power steering failures occurred with some frequency.

Not least of all, the hood latch was known to fail, allowing the hood to pop up unexpectedly—a blinding and potentially deadly flaw. The catalytic converter flange was prone to crack, and the carburetor lean/rich computer was prone to

error. The 1979 models added electrical system failures to this list of woes, and capped that with unreliable differentials.

Wheel bearing seizures and a tendency for both front doors to jam in 35-mph (56-kph) crash tests were two new bad features that the 1980 models added to the entirety of Aspen/Volare problems. The year 1980 was the last year that these cars were produced.

There were also those large cars that sought to become ecnomical—if not through sheer leanness of diet, then through the cheapness of the fuels consumed. In the great rush for fuel economy in the 1970s, the diesel engine achieved a popularity that was to last into the 1980s.

While dieselization did not have quite the revolutionary effect it had on railroads—in which the previous form of motive power was entirely supplanted—the rattle of solid valve lifters was soon heard from nearly as many cars as trucks: a sure sign that the diesel automotive engine had come of age.

1978–83 General Motors 350-cubic-inch (5.7-liter) diesels

General Motors was one of the first companies to join the happy diesel throng, offering diesel engine options on

a number of its upscale model lines. However, someone at GM authorized the conversion of a 350-cubic-inch (5.7-liter) gasoline engine for use in some of these diesel models.

This was unfortunate because the diesel principal is one that requires very high compression to make its slow-burning fuel work to power a vehicle. The diesel piston's forte is the long, powerful push—as opposed to the quick 'punching' action of gasoline pistons.

Therefore, the diesel engine has to be built heavier, to withstand the high compression and extended duration of its 'power strokes.' A converted gasoline engine is simply too puny to handle the extended diesel pressures.

So, this conversion attempt failed. The cars afflicted with these unsuccessful hybrids were middle-size to large 1978–83 models with wheelbases upwards of 115 inches (2.9 meters), and styling that generally included two- and four-door sedans and two-door coupes. Basically, that meant all 1978–83 General Motors diesel-engined cars with 350-cubic-inch (5.7-liter) engines.

Such engines were offered for the 1978–83 Buick Electra, Le Sabre, Regal and Riviera; 1978–83 Cadillac De Ville, Eldorado, Fleetwood and Seville; 1978–1983 Chevrolet Caprice, Impala, Malibu and Monte Carlo; 1978–83 Oldsmobile Cutlass, Cutlass Supreme, Delta Eighty-Eight, Ninety-Eight, and Toronado; and 1978–83 Pontiac Bonneville, Catalina, Grand Prix and Le Mans.

Thus, these cars, when equipped with

the 350-cubic-inch (5.7-liter) diesel engine, had serious powerplant problems (of course)—including broken crankshafts and cracked engine blocks, as well as fuel pump, head gasket and fuel injector failures.

An additional problem was that the *faux diesel* (to coin a term) 350-cubic-inch (5.7-liter) engines were mated to a transmission that became a legend for its imperfections—the THM 200 automatic. This is the transmission about which the California Attorney General's Office stated that (like the Federal Trade Commission), they had received 'more individual consumer complaints...than any other automotive transmission in history.'

Among the 1978–83 General Motors cars that were available with the 350-ci (5.7-liter) diesel was the elegantly trim Cadillac Seville (at top, above).

It was far better to order the Seville with a slightly more fuel-expensive gasoline engine than that particular disastrous diesel—not to mention foregoing the W-31 automatic transmission, which was almost as bad as the diesel.

Above: Another of the upper-level 1978–83 cars for which the 350-ci (5.7-liter) diesel was available—a 1978 Buick Electra.

Overleaf: A 350-ci (5.7 liter) diesel V-8-equipped 1982 Oldsmobile Cutlass. Again, for the owner of this car, a gasoline V-8 would have served better.

DUBIOUS CARS OF THE FUTURE

H aving covered some of the mistakes and misunderstandings of automotive endeavor up to the early 1980s, one might be tempted to pass immediate judgement on the remainder of the 1980s as well.

However, some things take time, and a retrospective approach is most commonly agreed upon to be the best when evaluating anything so near to the heart of the average motorist as the automobile that he or she may own.

We already have a 'lock-in' with the aged and smoke-belching Trabant (please see the text on that car)—a vehicle that has been manufactured throughout three decades, and was a marginal vehicle at its inception.

Would it indeed be fair to place the tag of 'worst' or 'bad' on such as the Suzuki Samurai, an all-terrain car that has its roots in the venerable US Army Jeep? The Samurais of the mid-1980s were alleged to have a propensity to roll over on slight inclines, but the facts on this are still being gathered.

The Yugo, an eastern Europen import of the latter 1980s, may also be a candidate for this future list—with Western drivers so far unimpressed by this product of the changing socialist state of Yugoslavia. While the Yugo seemed like a good deal, with pricing that was low enough to be considered a 'steal' no matter the quality of the car, some owners feel that it is not a reliable car, and perhaps is far less of a bargain than its sticker price would indicate.

A new import in the 1980s was the Yugo, a Yugoslavian car built in the then-popular hatchback 'econobox' design format.

While not a bad car per se, Yugo service was hard to get—not a good selling point for a mass-market automobile—and there were owner complaints about the car's operating efficiency. These are not reasons to call the Yugo a 'lemon,' but who knows what history will reveal?

Below: A Yugo hatchback sedan.

Then again, a case could be made for a four-wheel-drive vehicle, designed specifically for off-road travel, that has a tendency to roll over easily.

So the newspapers proclaimed the flaws of the Suzuki Samurai in the mid-1980s. However, Suzuki countered with their 'consumer protection package,' and insufficient time has passed to warrant a 'thumbs up' or 'thumbs down.'

Opposite: A mid-1980s Suzuki Samurai.

This leads us to focus on the relative dearth of Yugo dealers in Western urban areas, which in turn brings up another question—when does difficulty of maintenance enter into the equation? For instance, the Ferrari Testarossa is a car that is arguably difficult to maintain, and requires specialized knowledge to do so, but could not seriously be included on a 'worst' list except under the 'luggage space' category.

Exclusivity is not a qualification. Besides, the creation of a true performance car for 'everyman' has been a frontier that has been breached again and again. The first Ford Thunderbird and the Triumph TR2 approached the situation from opposite ends of the spectrum.

The Thunderbird was not an exceptionally good handling machine, but was meant to impress, and while it did not handle appreciably worse or better than many other cars of its period, it could out-accelerate many of them.

The Triumph was underpowered enough for its handling characteristics, was never billed as an all-out race car, and never pretended to be one—but it gave the average sportscar novice a taste of what the 'real thing' might be like. Troubles sometimes haunt such endeavors, however.

Therefore, the popular and sprightly Pontiac Fiero, a 1980s American knockoff of the mid-engine Fiat X-1/9, suffered some engine compartment fire problems with its four-cylinder (as opposed to trouble-free six-cylinder) models. Even so, will this car be present on any 'worst list' of the future?

In the long perspective down the years, will current attempts at all-wheel-drive on the part of Audi, Honda, Subaru, Volkswagen and others produce a crop of cars that are unprecedented successes, abysmal failures, or cars that bring forth such a mass of technical complications that whole new horizons of mechanical failure (or success) are unveiled?

For all of these but the benighted Trabant, we will simply have to wait until the data is in. Until such time, we must look to the past—for those *successes that might have been* but for a *fatal flaw*, as well as for those that *never*, in anyone's wildest imagination, *could have been*.

These pages: *Pontiac Fieros. Some customers had engine-fire problems with early four-cylinder Fieros, but those who bought six-cylinder Fieros have not experienced same.*

Therefore, the Fiero is probably not a 'worst car' suspect—only time will tell.

BIBLIOGRAPHY

Berkebile, Donald H and Oliver, Smith Hempstone. *The Smithsonian Collection of Automobiles & Motorcycles*. Washington: Smithsonian, 1968.

Bird, Anthony. *Antique Automobiles*. New York: EP Dutton, 1967.

Borgeson, Griffith. 'Edmund Rumpler: Icarus Bound'; *Automobile Quarterly Vol 22, No 3*. Princeton: Automobile Quarterly, 1984.

Boyne, Walter J. *The Power Behind the Wheel*. New York: Stewart, Tabori & Chang, 1988.

Burke, John G and Eakin, Marshall C. *Technology and Change*. San Francisco: Boyd & Fraser, 1979.

Clutton, Cecil and Bird, Paul. *The Vintage Car Guide*. Garden City: Doubleday, 1976.

Clymer, Floyd. *Those Wonderful Old Automobiles*. New York: McGraw-Hill, 1953.

Clymer, Floyd. *Treasury of Early American Automobiles*. New York: McGraw-Hill, 1950.

Darack, Arthur. *The Used Car Book*. Englewood Cliffs: Prentice-Hall, 1983.

DeWaard, E John. *Fins & Chrome*. London: Bison Books Ltd, 1982.

The Editors of Consumer Automotive Press. *The Used Car Book*. New York: Ballantine, 1985.

Edmonston, Phil. *Lemon-Aid*. New York: Beaufort Books, 1981.

Fuller, R Buckminster and Marks, Robert. *The Dymaxion World of R Buckminster Fuller*. Garden City: Anchor/Doubleday, 1973.

Lawday, David. 'The Last Gasp for Another Wheezing Relic of Socialism'; *US News & World Report*, April 2, 1990. Washington: US News & World Report, 1990.

Nichols, Richard. *Classic American Cars*. London: Bison Books Ltd, 1986.

Porazik, Juraj. *Old Time Classic Cars*. New York: Arco, 1985.

Robson, Graham. *Pictorial History of the Automobile*. New York: Gallery, 1987.

Yenne, Bill. *World's Worst Aircraft*. London: Bison Books Ltd.

PICTURE CREDITS

INDEX

Below: *A Suzuki Samurai and its
sporty twin, the Sidekick, follow
a rugged wilderness trail. The
history of motoring has been
just such a winding and dust-
obscured path. One can seldom
tell what lies ahead—and what
has happened behind can only
be discerned 'after the dust
settles.'*